Sporting Capital

In a world of competing public policy priorities, economic challenges and political uncertainty, sports development organisations and initiatives need to adapt to survive. This book makes the case for 'Sporting Capital' as a new conceptual model of sports participation with the potential to transform public policy and practice in sports development.

The central argument presented is that a model of Sporting Capital – with its three domains of physiological, social and psychological attributes – provides a missing framework, creating a new impetus for sustained growth in community sport by joining up the levels at which sports development is planned and implemented. Touching on important issues such as youth sport, public health, volunteering, disability, ethnicity and social inequality, it examines patterns of sports participation in relation to age, gender and social class and offers recommendations for strategic policy improvements that can be implemented by practitioners working on the front line of community sport.

Sporting Capital: Transforming Sports Development Policy and Practice provides valuable insights for all those interested in sports development, youth sport, community sport, or sport and social policy.

Nicholas F. Rowe is a freelance sport research consultant and Visiting Research Fellow at Leeds Becket University, UK. For nearly 30 years he worked for the GB Sport Council and Sport England, most recently as Sport England's Strategic Lead for Research and Evaluation.

Routledge Research in Sport, Culture and Society

www.routledge.com/sport/series/RRSCS

Sporting Capital

Transforming Sports Development Policy and Practice

Nicholas F. Rowe

Routledge
Taylor & Francis Group

LONDON AND NEW YORK

First published 2018
by Routledge
2 Park Square, Milton Park, Abingdon, Oxon OX14 4RN

and by Routledge
711 Third Avenue, New York, NY 10017

Routledge is an imprint of the Taylor & Francis Group, an informa business

British Library Cataloguing-in-Publication Data
A catalogue record for this book is available from the British Library

Library of Congress Cataloging-in-Publication Data
A catalog record for this book has been requested

ISBN: 978-1-138-29017-4 (hbk)
ISBN: 978-1-315-26650-3 (ebk)

Typeset in Sabon
by Apex CoVantage, LLC

To Sally and Thomas

Contents

Figures

Preface

Sport has always featured not just as an important part of my life but as something that has defined and shaped it. It has been integral to my sense of who I am and what I do. It has given me, and continues to give me, a deep unending well of enjoyment from both the pleasure of playing and from the camaraderie of time spent with people who share that pleasure with me. Beyond dominating my spare time leisure activities, I have been fortunate enough for sport to reach into my professional career having worked for nearly 30 years in a national strategic sports development organisation and now as a consultant to influence and shape community sport-related research.

Reflecting on my own biography, my earliest memories are of my father playing football, my mother winning the 'Mum's race' at our primary school sports day and sport in all its shapes and forms being a constant topic of family conversation. As I reached junior and then secondary school age I was picked to play in a wide range of school teams, played and watched football with my Dad and spent most of my spare time outdoors either hitting or kicking a ball. In my mid teens I encouraged my Dad to play golf with me and he never looked back!

At University I found many distractions that temporarily took me away from regularly playing sports but always knew that I would return to take part when the time was right. As I got older my interests shifted from team sports to marathon running and to playing golf. And now in my retirement from full time working I have found time to challenge myself in new ways by cycling around the coast of Britain, keeping myself ticking over with regular 'jogs' in the countryside and spending even more time at my local golf club playing, officiating and contributing in various voluntary capacities.

Why am I sharing this with you? It is to make the important point that my experience is far from unique. Hundreds of thousands of people in this country and millions of others worldwide have had the same experience of sport in their lives and for a relatively small number participation in sport has been their source of income and livelihood. I suspect, like me, they never really questioned from a personal biographical perspective why sport in all its forms from participating to spectating at live events, from watching on television to reading in newspapers and, for me, 'researching' and writing a book about it, came to be so central in our lives.

But what made it unthinkable for me that I wouldn't be taking part in sport throughout my life? At a personal level for many years it was a question that I never really dwelt upon. However, in my professional capacity the question of what distinguished people like me who find it difficult to stop taking part in sport from those who it is almost impossible to make participate began over recent years to dominate my thinking. This thinking culminated in my ideas around 'sporting capital'. Sport is a central part of my life and something that has given me so much enjoyment only because I have had the capacities to enjoy it and to get the most from it. Those capacities are not simple or easy to define but they may be summarised into the three 'Cs' of competence, confidence and connections. My early life experience, in the family, at school and with my peers equipped me with the basic skills and confidence needed to enjoy a wide range of sports. My experience over the years has built on that foundation to provide positive and reinforcing feedback that has maintained and enhanced this 'stock' of capacities. I have drawn on this stock to overcome the constraints and barriers that life can put in the way. The motivation to take part in sport has prevailed in the face of all the obstacles thrown at me at different stages in my life.

However, my experience is not universal. For far too many, sport is something they find threatening, difficult, intimidating and unrewarding. It is something they tolerated at school but as soon as the opportunity arose it is something of which they steered well clear. For many others sport was something that was ok to do when they were young but wasn't sufficiently enjoyable to prioritise and persist with into adulthood. Their stock of capacities to take part in sport were low and over time got lower still as they became more socially and physically distanced from sport as an active pursuit. For people like me it is difficult to understand how these people feel about sport. In a public policy context there is a danger that this lack of empathy is institutionalised in the organisations that are run by sport enthusiasts who believe that everyone would take part in sport if only the opportunity was made available to them.

It was the realisation, informed by a combination of personal and professional experience, that the motivation to take part in sport is driven by a kind of invisible 'capital' that people carry around with them that started to open my eyes to the power of this idea. That this capital is similar in kind and connected to other cultural, social and human capitals helped the idea take form and develop. In this book I have sought to take the idea of sporting capital and build it into a coherent theoretical framework that I believe has the potential to create a paradigm shift in the way public policy for community sport is conceived and implemented. I say this advisedly and without in any way seeking to diminish the challenges involved of which I am fully aware.

Writing this book has involved a journey of self reflection, critical analysis and a test of logic and personal application. The ideas expressed are in no way meant as a denunciation of all the efforts of those who have worked in sports development over the last 40 years or so, including of course my own. In fact there are many examples over those years where interventions have embraced aspects of sporting capital without assigning that label to them and without being interpreted and understood within its wider theoretical framework. However, I do believe that public policy has been held back in its potential effectiveness by lacking the coherent theoretical framework that sporting capital offers. And I believe that application of the theory could have a transformative impact on how we prioritise interventions in sport, how we design those interventions and crucially how we train and educate the workforce both paid and voluntary who are at the forefront of delivering on those interventions.

In this book I have talked about an ambition of 'sporting capital for all'. It is a vision where everyone no matter what age, what background or gender has the basic physical skills to take part in sport in ways that are rewarding, has the self confidence and 'can do' attitude that motivates and maintains participation throughout their lives and has access to the social connections and reinforcing social contexts that values and supports participation. In an ideal world these physically, sport literate people will have high quality infrastructure and environments that support and nurture their engagement. Those who chose not to take part in sport perhaps because they see other aspects of their lives and use of their capabilities in those areas more rewarding will make that choice from a position of strength and not weakness. This is to view sporting capital as a form of empowerment and not as one of individual deficit or limitation.

My ambition in this book has been to challenge received wisdom by starting a debate that will lead to change. There are many routes by which change can occur. It can be bottom up or top down, it can be directive or experiential, it can be incremental or revolutionary. This book is far from definitive on this count. Sporting capital as a theory is not fully tested and many of its propositions require further research. However, I believe a synthesis of the evidence available supports its plausibility and potential to breathe new life and sense of purpose into community sports development and enhance its justification in a world of competing priorities and challenging public policy environments. I hope at the very least that the readers of this book will reflect on its key messages to challenge their ways of thinking, how they behave and relate to others in their own personal lives and, if like me they are fortunate enough to work in community sports development, to help shape and influence what they do professionally to bring about transformative change.

Nicholas F. Rowe

Acknowledgements

The antecedents to this book go back a long way. It would not have been possible without the good fortune I had to be recruited as a research assistant many, many years ago at the then G. B. Sports Council by Mike Collins and Arthur Dye. I couldn't have asked for better mentors to induct me into the world of sport, social policy and research. They are both sorely missed and I owe them a great debt of gratitude.

My colleagues over many years in the Sport England Research Team have all played their part – they know who they are and it would not be right for me to single them out. But I thank them all for their inspiration, support, intelligence and dedication. They were influential in shaping the ideas that I have presented in this book, wittingly or unwittingly, although I absolve them of any responsibility for them.

In the nearly 30 years I worked in national sports research my paths crossed with many inspirational people. There are four, however, that I would like to thank in particular, Professors Chris Gratton, Peter Taylor, Fred Coalter and Jonathan Long. In their own inimitable ways they have all influenced and challenged me over the years, although I would also like to think that at times I might have challenged them.

I would like to express my thanks to StreetGames UK and in particular to Ceris Anderson and Jane Ashworth for their support in commissioning the original research that made this book possible. The primary research reported in Chapters 6 and 7 draws heavily on earlier work I carried out for them (www.streetgames.org/resource/sporting-capital-and-doorstep-sport-working-build-legacy-sports-participation-england) and I appreciate their permission to use it in the context of this book. I would also like to thank Oliver Nordern and Joel Williams who while at TNS-BMRB carried out the modelling work to build the Sporting Capital Index.

My thanks also to Leeds Beckett University where in my position as a Visiting Research Fellow they have given me access to their bibliographic resources without which this book would not have been possible. Also thanks to Simon Whitmore, Cecily Davey and the team at Routledge for having the vision that a book on Sporting Capital was possible and helping me bring it to fruition.

Last but not least I would like to thank Sally Hall as a sounding board for my ideas, for putting up with my need for constant approval and for bringing her librarian skills to bear on helping me with the task of referencing and indexing material.

Chapter 1

Introduction

This book is about an idea. The idea is conceptualised in two simple words, 'sporting capital'. But contained in these two words are multiple layers of meaning that span subject matter as diverse as individual human behaviour, motivational psychology, physical motor development, pedagogy, political sciences, philosophy, cultural studies and social policy. Sporting capital is not an abstract idea, but is an idea with a purpose in the sense that it is 'a thought or suggestion as to a possible course of action'. In writing this book I have taken the germ of this idea to build a coherent theory defined as 'a set of principles on which the practice of an activity is based'. Theories evolve and are there to be tested and challenged in the real world. The theory of sporting capital provides a framework for empirical research and a guide to policy and action. It is a theory that is very much in its infancy insofar as it has yet to undergo thorough 'road testing'; but all theories have to start somewhere, and those putting them forward must, with an open mind, be prepared to take some bumps and bruises along the way. As we go down that road I anticipate healthy and constructive criticism but am optimistic that sporting capital will emerge as a theory whose time has come.

In the contested world of 'sports development' (Houlihan and White, 2002; Collins, 2010a; Houlihan and Green, 2011; Hylton, 2013) I have come to the view, after more than 25 years of working at a national level bridging public policy and research, that the lack of a coherent theoretical foundation has limited its impact and by inference undermined its justification. These may be harsh words, but the evidence, referred to in Chapter 2, of the decades of stagnation in participation rates in sport and the apparent inability of governments, policy makers and practitioners to make significant inroads into structural social inequalities associated with age, gender, class, ethnicity and disability support this contention. This is despite substantial investment of public monies combined with the undoubted efforts of many well-meaning individuals, amongst whom I include myself, who believe and continue to believe in the transformative power of sport, the justification for state intervention and its ability to make a difference. Coalter (2007b, p. 7) makes reference to the need to "de-mythologize sport" and refers to "the sport evangelists who have invested much in their professional repertoires". In this book I am replacing this fuzzy mythological and evangelical narrative policy framework with one that is coherent, testable, capable of rational argument and, crucially, offers the potential to deliver results on the ground. In doing so I am hoping to take the surplus emotional power of sport and all those who promote it and harness it into a shared and effective theoretical framework for action.

I am aware that sporting capital as a theory will be open to the academic challenge of being reductionist in the pejorative sense of this word. And yes, it is possible to present sporting capital as a straightforward intuitively attractive idea. However, rather than apologising for its simplicity I would argue that this is a necessary attribute if theory is to be translated into an effective call for action. The apparent simplicity of the theory is, I believe, a strength and not a weakness. I would counter the reductionist argument by contending that behind its simplicity the theory is embedded with a sophisticated recognition of the complex systems (multiple not singular) that impact and interact to shape human sporting behaviour. At one level sporting capital is a micro theory that relates to the individual, his or her identity, predispositions, motivations, personal qualities, physiology and preferences. At a meso level sporting capital is about parental, family and peer influence, local institutional contexts, pedagogical frameworks, neighbourhoods and communities and local environments. At a macro level it is about broader socio-cultural contexts, shared value systems, national identities, public welfare and quality of life. In this sense sporting capital may be characterised as spanning and synthesising a 'society in leisure' approach which draws on structural forms of explanation and a socio-psychological approach that focuses on individual motivations, benefits and satisfactions (Coalter, 1997).

This intersection of disciplines and geographies is, I believe, an inherent strength of the theory. But it poses in turn a particular challenge for the author. I do not claim expertise across this multiplicity of disciplines, very few if any could, and I apologise in advance to any readers with specialist knowledge in any given area. My ambition in this book is big but it is limited. It is to provide an introductory narrative, supported by an initial foray into empirical evidence, for the idea of sporting capital at a level that is intellectually sound, intuitively compelling and that translates into an agenda for change and action. In order to do this I weave together a number of threads from a range of disciplines but only insofar as they are relevant to my general thesis on sporting capital. Readers who want text book, discursive and or critical overviews in say the political context of sport development and its history (Houlihan, 1997; Gratton and Henry, 2001; Houlihan and White, 2002; Houlihan, 2014; Houlihan and Lindsey, 2014; Grix and Phillpots, 2014; Grix, 2016), the psychology of sport, exercise and physical activity (Biddle and Mutrie, 2008; Weinberg and Gould, 2015), the sociology of sport (Giulianotti, 2005; Maguire et al., 2002; Jarvie and Thornton, 2012), sport pedagogy (Kirk, Macdonald and O'Sullivan, 2006; Tinning, 2008; Armour, 2013) and international comparative experience (Van Bottenburg, Rijnen and van Sterkenburg, 2005; Nicholson, Hoye and Houlihan, 2011; Hoekman, Breedveld and Scheerder, 2011; Van Bottenburg and De Bosscher, 2011; Hallmann and Petry, 2013) should look elsewhere.

My hope is that those in the academic world pick up the gauntlet to establish an evidence base that challenges and builds the theory in the contexts and disciplines in which their expertise lies, and ideally in multi and interdisciplinary collaborative research frameworks. But beyond this, and crucially linked to it, my ultimate ambition, and the reason I have written this book, is the hope that the theory will be used in applied settings by those who shape local policy and practice and by those who deliver it at the 'front line'. Their experience of how the theory can be applied to practice, what works, how and why and in what context is crucial and I pick this issue up in the final chapter. I am a realist, however, and although I would prefer to see a national sport development framework with sporting capital at its core driven by a growing evidence base, I recognise that change in this direction, if it occurs at all, is likely to be a slow, messy and incremental process. My experience to date in sharing my ideas with local sports development practitioners, for example in South and West Yorkshire, has been a positive one stimulating constructive debate and an appetite to translate the theory into practice. It encourages me to believe that a 'bottom up' approach, if that is indeed what is required, to influence a paradigm shift in national policy is certainly not out of the question.

Of course some would say that sporting capital is not a new idea, and I would agree that none of its constituent parts are 'new'. Other researchers have emphasised the interdependencies and impact of intrapersonal, biological/physical, psychological, social and structural/ecological factors in the decision to participate in sport (see for example: Henderson, 2009; Sallis, Owen and Fisher, 2008; Bailey et al., 2010). Stuij (2015) in research on the impact of different social class backgrounds on young people's socialisation into sport makes reference to 'sporting capital' as a form of cultural capital linking it to Bourdieu's concept of the habitus. It would be surprising if nearly half a century of public policy focus and research had not yielded such insights and relationships. I do believe, however, that as a coherent theoretical perspective that can facilitate a radical shift in public policy, sporting capital theory as presented here brings something significant and new to the table. In Chapter 4 I examine other theories that have at times surfaced in the policy context of sport, and conclude that at best they are partial, in some cases more descriptive than explanatory and in others cases ill-fitting when borrowed from other fields, particularly and currently, those of behaviour change and physical activity.

In the 28 years I worked at Sport England rarely did a month pass where we didn't have anguished discussions about the scope and meaning of the word 'sport'. As Coalter (2007b, p. 7) says, "sport is a collective noun which hides much more than it reveals. . . . There are almost endless variations of sport processes, mechanisms, participants and experiences". The COMPASS project (UK Sport, 1999), examining comparative participation rates in different European countries, found that one of the greatest conceptual and practical difficulties encountered in attempting to make meaningful international comparisons of participation in sport concerns the way sport is defined. These national variations in definition are as much a consequence of cultural differences in the understanding of what sport is as they are about how the measurement of sport is operationalised. Van Bottenburg, Rijnen and van Sterkenburg (2005, p. 15) in their analysis of sport trends across the European Union made the observation that,

> Sport has become a strongly differentiated and diffuse phenomenon, which is practiced for many different ends, in diverse ways and in divergent contexts and organisational forms. How people experience sport is also related to this. More than ever before, people have the tendency to label their activities as 'sport'. This is furthered by the fact that sport has been 'upgraded' in both a social and cultural sense during the past few decades. One of the consequences of this is that sport in the year 2004 encompasses a broad spectrum with the Olympic games at one extreme, as the ultimate manifestation of organised competitive sport, and at the other, all kinds of physical activity that people (in contrast to fifty years ago) perceive as sporting behaviour.

Variously through the last 30 years or so the scope and definition of sport in England, at least as it applies to government policy, intervention and measurement, has swung between a very wide one that encompasses practically anything that moves (Council of Europe, 1992) to one that is more narrowly defined to exclude for example walking and certain types of cycling and or certain types of games such as darts or other activities that didn't meet thresholds of physical intensity (Sport England, 2004, 2008). Of course there is no absolute right or wrong answer. As referenced above, sport is a cultural phenomenon; for example in some countries bridge, a card game, and chess, a board game, are defined as sport, in Finland 'hunting moose' is a sporting activity. However, the scope of the definition of sport in a policy context cannot be ignored as it impacts on its policy leverage and impact. For example a very wide definition of sport embracing physical activity extends its relevance to public health and specifically to the obesity policy domain increasing potential funding opportunities and political influence. However, such a wide definition also increases the potential for sport policy to lose its focus, to dilute its impact by spreading investment too thinly and to undermine its relationships with its more traditional core constituencies and stakeholders. These tensions and dilemmas undoubtedly go a long way to explain the yo-yoing of national sport policy over the last 30 years or so between 'big sport' and 'smaller sport' policy domains.

It is important that I make clear from the outset that sporting capital is unapologetically a 'sport policy theory' rather than a physical activity theory. The salience of the theory to sport is its strength, not its weakness. One of the three pillars (domains) of sporting capital is the social connections that people have in and through sport which in turn encompasses the institutional context for sport in the broadest sociological sense. Sporting capital as a theoretical construct applies in particular, but not exclusively, to all 'organised sport' even if that organisation is limited and outside of for example a formal club setting. It includes in its scope team sports, individual sports, recreational walking, recreational cycling, road running and a wide range of health and fitness activities. However, it is less applicable to physical activities where the motivation is concerned with other instrumental outcomes such as DIY or housework, transport as a primary purpose, gardening or other hobbies or artistic activities that have a physical component (see Khan et al., 2012, p. 60 for a useful conceptual model of the relationship between sport, exercise and physical activity). Although sporting capital has an application to elite sport performance insofar as a pre-condition of becoming an elite athlete is an initial developmental process to build high levels of sporting capital, the focus of the theory is not at this level. It is, however, worth noting the link made in Chapter 3 where I discuss the transferability of 'capitals' and how, for elite professional sports people, sporting capital becomes one and the same as 'human capital' insofar as it is marketable and acquires economic value.

The apparent cyclical shifts in how sport is defined in public policy have been at least matched by the concurrent shifts in the rationale for public investment in sport (see for example: Coalter, Long and Duffield,1988; Coalter, 2007a; Coalter, 2007b; DCMS and Strategy Unit, 2002; Collins, 2010b; Grix and Carmichael, 2012). It could be argued that the justification for public investment in reality lies somewhere on a spectrum between at one end what has been termed 'sport for sports sake' to at the other end 'sport for good' i.e. sport as an instrumental means to achieve other social, educational, economic and public health outcomes. The political context in which sport policy is acted out has perhaps inevitably presented national sport policy as unequivocally at one or other end of this spectrum although the reality is always more nuanced. Hylton and Totten (2008) suggest that sports development intervention exists along a continuum that ranges from at one extreme an emphasis that is purely sport-related development outcomes to at the other extreme initiatives that are predominantly focused on community well-being. It could be argued that this politicisation process of sport policy with five to 10 yearly seismic shifts in positioning, at least in the rhetoric of sport if less in the reality, has worked to the overall detriment of achieving sustained impacts on mass participation or delivering wider public policy outcomes (Houlihan, 2011; Collins, 2010b).

Recent experience is illustrative. Sport England was categorical in its '2008 to 11 Strategy' that it was 'sport first' and 'health and other outcomes second',

> In the future Sport England's role will be to focus exclusively on sport. Sport can and does play a major role in achieving wider social and economic benefits – notably on the health front. However, the driving force behind the strategy and investment is to address the needs of sport participants across the country. This provides a clear distinction with the physical activity agenda being driven by a number of departments, including the Department of Health and Department of Transport.
>
> (Sport England, 2008, p. 1)

Eight years on, post the London Olympic Games and missed sport participation legacy targets, the latest Government and Sport England strategies (H. M. Government, 2015; Sport England, 2016) have swung the pendulum firmly back towards both a very wide definition of 'sport', which extends well into the informal domain of physical activity, and an instrumental 'sport for good' orientation. This shift is presented unequivocally by the Minister for Sport in her foreword where she states,

> At the heart of this new strategy sit five simple but fundamental outcomes: physical health, mental health, individual development, social and community development and economic development. It is these outcomes that will define who we fund, what we fund and where our priorities lie in future. It sets the pathway for sport and physical activity for the next decade and beyond.
>
> (H. M. Government, 2015, p. 1)

An outside interested observer might be less sanguine about the longevity of this newest emphasis in public policy for sport.

It is important to understand where sporting capital theory sits in relation to these changing policy contexts. We need to be clear that 'sporting capital' exists in the same way that say human capital exists, independent of whether government prioritises it, invests in it, values it in its own right or values it as a means to achieving something else. Sporting capital provides the fundamental building blocks that underpin individual motivation to take part in sport. Whether the rationale stops at sport for its own sake or extends beyond this to sport for good, building sporting capital is the primary means to achieving both these ends and in the latter case has the added benefits associated with the transferability of capitals. The simple logic is as follows:

government intervention to increase sporting capital and extend its reach to a wider cross section of people leads to more sustained participation which in turn leads to improved health, education, social cohesion, economic benefit and so on. Of course this simple logic is in reality far from simple and is beset with issues of cause and effect, claims, counter claims and 'over claims' and with what Coalter (2007b) has termed the issue of 'necessary and sufficient conditions'.

The principal position that I take in this book is that: 1) having the requisite level of sporting capital is a necessary condition to participate in sport at all and particularly to do so over the life-course; 2) that, left to their own devices most people in advantageous social, economic and cultural contexts will build high levels of sporting capital and participate in sport regularly throughout their lives with all the attendant benefits that this brings; 3) that many people in less advantageous circumstances will live their lives having never achieved the levels of sporting capital that makes participation in sport an attractive proposition that sustains their interest and engagement; 4) that many more who achieve modest levels of sporting capital experience slow attrition in those levels over time as age, life transitions and external barriers intervene to the point that militates against participation; and 5) that public policy intervention can, if directed in the right way, lift the level of sporting capital amongst those who would otherwise fall below the threshold required to engage or re-engage in active and sustained participation in sport.

The focus of this book is on sport policy in England and that is where the majority of my personal experience lies. However, over the years in the context of my research with Sport England I have been engaged in extensive European wide debates on sport policy particularly as it impacts on levels and patterns of sport participation and related social trends (UK Sport, 1999). Where appropriate I occasionally refer to these wider European experiences and draw on evidence from outside Europe. For those readers from beyond these shores I would emphasise the universal nature of sporting capital as a theoretical construct. Although socio-cultural contexts vary from country to country, the building blocks of sporting capital as they apply to each individual remain the same albeit with limitless permutations. However, to the extent that levels of participation in sport are different in different countries it is reasonable to postulate that overall aggregate levels of sporting capital also vary. In Chapter 6 I present statistics on the levels of sporting capital in England. My hypothesis, as yet untested, is that a similar study in say Sweden, Finland, Denmark or Norway where participation rates are higher than in England would reveal higher aggregate levels of sporting capital across the population and importantly higher levels amongst women, ethnic minorities and lower socio-economic groups. Once established, unpicking and understanding the root causes of these differences would provide useful comparative insights that could support more effective public policy intervention in all countries concerned and I discuss this more fully in Chapter 9.

I firmly believe that there are clear, tangible recommendations emerging from sporting capital theory that are relevant to policy and practice. At a macro level the theory challenges prevailing policy emphases that have focused on supply, increasing opportunity, simplistic views on social marketing, the impact of major events and influence of role models, at the expense of more sophisticated demand side and individual capacity building intervention. The theory also has a lot to say about the structural inequalities in sports participation that relate in particular to social class and gender and their antecedents. At a micro level, through better profiling and assessment of individual levels of sporting capital, project designers and practitioners will be better able to intervene in ways that engage and meet individual needs based on current levels of sporting capital (see Chapters 8 and 9). This will impact, for example, on the types of sports and fitness activities offered, the style of delivery, including levels of competition and emphasis on intrinsic and or extrinsic motivational delivery, and the mix of gender and abilities in groups and teams. At its heart, however, sporting capital theory is not just a theory confined to individual behaviour change but embraces a system wide approach to intervention which integrates national policy with social and environmental circumstances, institutional frameworks and personal values, beliefs and traits (see Chapter 3). To this extent sporting capital theory sits within the broader socio-ecological model of behaviour referenced earlier in this chapter.

It is important to clarify what may be considered omissions from this book. The theory of sporting capital is, I would contend, a universal one insofar as whatever the context and circumstances that might apply sporting capital exists as embodied characteristics and capacities that impact on an individual's sporting behaviours. Everybody has a certain level of sporting capital although the permutations of the building blocks of that capital in relation to the psychological, physiological and social attributes and capabilities are unlimited. In this book I have focused my attention on the relationship between sporting capital, age, gender and social class as significant structural factors in society with known relationships to participation in sport. I have purposefully omitted any detailed reference to the importance and impact of sporting capital on sporting behaviours of people with a disability not because I in any way have placed this as a lower priority but because I would be unable to do the subject matter justice in the context of this book. I have in Chapter 9 made reference to the importance of prioritising research to further explore this relationship between sporting capital and participation in sport. Similarly I have omitted specific exploration or empirical analysis of the relationship between sporting capital and participation in sport by people from different ethnic groups or of people with different sexual orientations. Again this is not to deny or devalue that relationship or its importance as an area of public policy but has been made to avoid drawing superficial conclusions particularly where they are limited by the empirical measures that define these groups in standardised ways that do not reflect their homogeneity and the different cultural contexts that influence their behaviours. This concern is highlighted by Long et al. (2009, p. 57) in their systematic review of the literature on Black and other ethnic minorities and sport,

> The constant cry from the researchers is for policymakers to recognise such differences and not treat minority ethnic groups as a homogeneous category. In particular the research stresses the importance of listening more closely to particular cultural and religious needs, such as those of some South Asian women, while recognising that these needs are not representative of all South Asian women.

In closing this introduction let us not forget in our academisation of sport that at a recreational and mass participation level it is driven by the sheer pleasure and enjoyment it brings. Enjoyment is derived from the mastery of skills, by overcoming personal challenges, stretching oneself physically and mentally, working collaboratively as part of a team or just being with friends and, for some, from satisfaction and or status associated with competitive success. (Wankel and Kreisel, 1985). Tay and Diener (2011, p. 363) in their empirical analysis of needs and subjective well-being (SWB) across a sample of 123 countries concluded that, "people need to fulfill a variety of needs, it is likely that a mix of daily activities that includes mastery, social relationships, and the meeting of physical needs is required for optimal SWB." Wankel (1993) suggested that an emphasis on enjoyment of LTPA (leisure-time physical activity) may have significant positive outcomes in two ways. One is its importance to leisure-time physical activity adherence and the second is through countering stress and facilitating positive psychological health. When sport ceases to be enjoyable, it is likely to cease to be a leisure choice. It is my contention that having high levels of sporting capital is fundamentally linked to the enhanced capacity for sport to be enjoyable and that achieving high levels of sporting capital is within the reach of most if not all individuals in developed societies. Achieving high levels of capital including human, social, cultural and sporting capital enhances the capacity for individuals to 'thrive' through self actualisation (Maslow, 1954), enhanced well-being and improved quality of life. It is linked to a philosophy of empowerment. Taking part in sport is always going to be a leisure choice, but it should be a choice made from a position of strength and capacity and not a negative one framed by limitation whether physical, psychological or social.

Structure of the book

Chapter 2. The public policy challenge for community sport: the need for a theoretically driven paradigm shift

This chapter sets up the central contention of the book that sports development, both as a profession and as a wider field of public policy, has lacked a coherent theoretical foundation for its work. It argues that having a more coherent and robust theory to underpin sports development policy and practice is not just a nice to have discourse for academic debate but a fundamental prerequisite for effective public policy. In setting up this argument the chapter includes a broad overview of the challenges that public policy ambitions for sport have faced since the Great Britain Sports Council was established in the early 1970s to the present day post London Olympic legacy concerns with sedentary behaviours and increasing levels of obesity. The argument is made that despite large amounts of public investment we have failed to 'shift the curve' of participation in sport in England or make significant inroads into structural inequalities. The chapter concludes by introducing the reader to the sporting capital conceptual model and proposing that 'sporting capital' offers a new lens on sport behaviours and their determinants that the author believes has the potential to unlock the door to improved understanding and in turn more effective public policy intervention that could transform the sporting landscape in England. The universal nature of sporting capital suggests that it could equally be applied to sports development policy and practice in other developed countries, albeit contextualised by their differing socio-economic, political and cultural contexts.

Chapter 3. Sporting capital – what is it, how does it relate to other forms of human, cultural and social capital and why is it important?

This chapter provides a detailed explanation of the theoretical construct of 'sporting capital' as "*the stock of physiological, social and psychological attributes and competencies that support and motivate an individual to participate in sport and to sustain that participation over time*" (Rowe, 2015, p 45). It explains how sporting capital theory is distinctive from, but related to, theories concerning human, cultural and social capital and explores the qualities that make them transferable. The model of sporting capital with its three domains of the physiological, psychological and social are explained and the theoretical propositions that underpin it are elaborated. The central contention that higher levels of sporting capital will predict both current and future participation probabilities is introduced. The proposition is made that people with high levels of sporting capital are much more likely to engage in lifelong participation than their peers with low levels of sporting capital. Other important characteristics of sporting capital that relate to public policy are introduced to include the relationship between sporting capital and barriers and constraints to participation and its relationship to health outcomes, volunteering and transferable skills.

Chapter 4. Theories of sport development and behaviour change – why do we need yet another theory?

This chapter addresses the potential challenge that rather than lacking a sound theoretical foundation, although invariably not made explicit, sports development policy and practice has over the years been influenced by a number of theoretical constructs. A brief review of each of these theories concludes that their application to the public policy domain of community sports development is a not a perfect fit. The 'sport theories' are orientated towards elite sport success and associated talent identification, development and pathways and say little about the determinants and influences that lead to inactivity, drop out from sport at an early age or a failure to sustain sporting activity through the life-course. The theories borrowed from the wider health and physical activity public policy domains have their strength in being grounded in the fundamental drivers and determinants of behaviour change but lack the cultural and institutional specificity that distinguishes sport from informal exercise and activity in everyday life. The chapter concludes that an effective theory of sporting behaviour and its determinants must embed the very nature of sport as a synthesis of the physiological, psychological and social realities that shape an individual's sporting behaviours within the cultural context in which they live. It argues that sporting capital does this by addressing the sport specific factors that are influential in both the decision to participate in sport at any given time and most importantly the likelihood of sustaining that participation over time.

Chapter 5. Sport participation over the life-course: linking the evidence to sporting capital theory

In this chapter I review the evidence on determinants of participation in sport across the life-course through the lens of sporting capital theory. In doing so I 'sense check' the theory and point towards the implications for policy and practice that flow from the new perspective it provides. This chapter takes the propositions that flow from the theory of sporting capital and explores the evidence that is relevant to those propositions. Central to the idea of sporting capital is the proposition that having more or less of it impacts not just on an individual's current probability of playing sport but also on the likely future prospects of sustaining participation into middle and older age. The orientation of this chapter is, therefore, to take a life-course approach to participation in sport, starting with what we know about the determinants of sport (and physical activity) in the very young, and reviewing the evidence of how early experiences impact on and track through into adulthood. The chapter includes sections on: 'sport through the life-course'; 'the early socialisation process – starting young'; 'the early learning motivational climate'; 'the importance of fundamental movement skills'; 'the importance of interpersonal relationships – socialisation beyond the family'; 'barriers and constraints – the context for participation'; and 'an ageing population – sport participation into older age'.

Chapter 6. Sporting capital in England: from measurement process to painting the landscape

This chapter explains the challenges involved in 'pinning down sporting capital' into a set of quantifiable measures. It explains how the theory was translated into an empirical model built and tested using primary survey data collected in Sport England's large-scale population-wide Active People Survey. The reader is introduced to a 10-point 'Sporting Capital Index' and the modelled relationship between sporting capital and participation rates in sport are demonstrated. Summary statistics are presented to provide a 'landscape' overview on the levels and distribution of sporting capital in England and the importance of the findings for policy and practice are highlighted.

Chapter 7. Sporting capital in England: understanding the impact of age, class, gender and sporting preferences

This chapter explores in more depth the distribution of sporting capital across different groups in the population, variations in the building blocks of sporting capital and the implication for levels of sustained participation in sport. It shows that there are structural variations in the levels of sporting capital that in turn explain variations in participation rates and raise broader concerns about the challenges involved for public policy. The second part of the chapter examines how people's frequency of participation in sport and the types of sports they are likely to participate in are affected by their levels of sporting capital. It shows how sports that are more competitive, technically demanding and requiring greater organisation are likely to be attractive to those with high levels of sporting capital but less so for those with low levels. A different sporting capital profile for 'fitness-related sports' shows them to offer a greater appeal as an entry into sport for those with low levels of sporting capital. The implications for the roles of national governing bodies of sport and for public policy more generally are discussed.

Chapter 8. Building sporting capital: applying the theory to policy and practice

This chapter takes the preceding theoretical and empirical discussion and explores the implications for policy and practice. At a macro level it explores the ingredients that might make up a national sport strategy that applies and structures its approach around the core theoretical constructs of sporting capital. This includes recommendations for the roles and responsibilities of the key agencies that impact on community sport outcomes and the implications for the 'agents of change' in the paid and voluntary workforce. At the micro level of project design and intervention it examines what this would look like if sporting capital 'principles' were applied and makes practical suggestions to help guide those in the front line of sports development. A brief exploration is made of the relevance and potential broader public policy application of sporting capital and its links through the transferability of capitals to wider social and health outcomes.

Chapter 9. Where do we go from here? Applying, refining and testing the model of sporting capital

Although acknowledged to be in its infancy, it is argued that sporting capital theory is plausible both in its internal logic and in its parallels with other well-established theories and concepts of human, cultural and social capital. Large claims are made for the potential impact sporting capital theory can have on public policy outcomes for sport. Initial empirical analysis has provided results that are promising and consistent with our broader understanding of the social profile of sport and the nature of differing sporting experiences. However, it is acknowledged that to become accepted as mainstream thinking to underpin public policy the theory requires to be systematically challenged, tested and refined through research. This chapter sets out a research agenda to include specific recommendations for 'strategic' research and for a programme of sporting capital-led intervention-based evaluative research to test and refine the theory in different settings to establish what works for whom and in what context. These settings could include comparative international research that might yield fascinating insights and explanations for the variability of sports participation across different countries. If successfully applied, sporting capital could become a universal language of sports development and the foundation for achieving our shared ambitions for sport in society.

References

Armour, K. ed., 2013. *Sport pedagogy: An introduction for teaching and coaching.* 2nd ed. London: Routledge.

Bailey, R., Collins, D., Ford, P., MacNamara, A., Toms, M. and Pearce, G., 2010. *Participant development in sport: An academic review.* Leeds: Sports Coach UK.

Biddle, S. J. H. and Mutrie, N., 2008. *Psychology of physical activity: Determinants, well-being and interventions.* 2nd ed. London: Routledge.

Coalter, F., 1997. Leisure sciences and leisure studies: Different concept, same crisis? *Leisure Sciences*, 19(4), pp. 255–268. http://dx.doi.org/10.1080/01490409709512254

Coalter, F., 2007a. Sports clubs, social capital and social regeneration: 'Ill-defined interventions with hard to follow outcomes'? *Sport in Society*, 10(4), pp. 537–559.

Coalter, F., 2007b. *A wider social role for sport: Who's keeping the score.* London: Routledge.

Coalter, F., Long, J. and Duffield, B., 1988. *Recreational welfare: The rationale for public sector investment in leisure.* Aldershot: Gower/Avebury.

Collins, M. ed., 2010a. *Examining sports development.* London: Routledge.

Collins, M., 2010b. From 'sport for good' to 'sport for sport's sake' – not a good move for sports development in England? *International Journal of Sport Policy*, 2(3), pp. 367–379.

Council of Europe, 1992. *European sports charter.* R (92) 13 Rev. Strasbourg: Council of Europe.

Department for Culture, Media and Sport and the Strategy Unit, 2002. *Game plan: A strategy for delivering government's sport and physical activity objectives.* London: Cabinet Office.

Giulianotti, R., 2005. *Sport, a critical sociology.* Cambridge: Polity Press.

Gratton, C. and Henry, I. P. eds., 2001. *Sport in the city: The role of sport in economic and social regeneration.* London: Routledge.

Grix, J., 2016. *Sport politics: An introduction.* London: Palgrave.

Grix, J. and Carmichael, F., 2012. Why do governments invest in elite sport? A polemic. *International Journal of Sport Policy and Politics*, 4(1), pp. 73–90.

Grix, J. and Phillpots, L. eds., 2014. *Understanding UK sport policy in context.* London: Routledge.

Hallmann, K. and Petry, K. eds., 2013. *Comparative sport development: Systems, participation and public policy.* New York: Springer.

Henderson, K. A., 2009. A paradox of sport management and physical activity interventions. *Sport Management Review*, 12(2), pp. 57–65.

H. M. Government, 2015. *Sporting future: A new strategy for an active nation.* London: Cabinet Office.

Hoekman, R., Breedveld, K. and Scheerder, J., 2011. Introduction to the Special Issue on Sports participation in Europe. *European Journal for Sport and Society*, 8(1-2) pp. 7–13.

Houlihan, B., 1997. *Sport, policy and politics: A comparative analysis.* London: Routledge.

Houlihan, B., 2011. England. In: M. Nicholson, R. Hoye, and B. Houlihan, eds. *Participation in sport, international policy perspectives.* London: Routledge. pp. 10–24.

Houlihan, B., 2014. *The government and politics of sport.* 2nd ed. London: Routledge.

Houlihan, B. and Green, M. eds., 2011. *Routledge handbook of sports development.* London: Routledge.

Houlihan, B. and Lindsey, I., 2014. *Sport policy in Britain.* London: Routledge.

Houlihan, B. and White, A., 2002. *The politics of sport development: Development of sport or development through sport?* London: Routledge.

Hylton, K. ed., 2013. *Sport development: Policy, process and practice.* 3rd ed. London: Routledge.

Hylton, K. and Totten, M., 2008. Community sports development. In: K. Hylton and P. Bramham, eds. *Sports development: Policy, process and practice.* New York: Routledge, pp. 77–117.

Jarvie, G. and Thornton, J., 2012. *Sport, culture and society: An introduction.* 2nd ed. London: Routledge.

Khan, K., Thompson, A., Blair, S., Sallis, J., Powell, K., Bull, F. and Bauman, A., 2012. Sport and exercise as contributors to the health of nations. *The Lancet,* 380(9836), pp. 59–64.

Kirk, D., Macdonald, D. and O'Sullivan, M., 2006. *The handbook of physical education.* London: Sage.

Long, J., Hylton, K., Spracklen, K., Ratna, A. and Bailey, S., 2009. *Systematic review of the literature on black and minority ethnic communities in sport and physical recreation.* London: Sport England.

Maguire, J., Jarvie, G., Mansfield, L. and Bradley, J. eds., 2002. *Sport worlds: A sociological perspective.* Champaign, IL: Human Kinetics.

Maslow, A. H., 1954. *Motivation and personality.* New York: Harper & Row.

Nicholson, M., Hoye, R. and Houlihan, B. eds., 2011. *Participation in sport: International perspectives.* London: Routledge.

Rowe, N. F., 2015. Sporting capital: A theoretical and empirical analysis of sport participation determinants and its application to sports development policy and practice. *International Journal of Sport Policy and Politics,* 7(1), pp. 43–61.

Sallis, J. F., Owen, N. and Fisher, E. B., 2008. Ecological models of health behavior. In: K. Glanz, B. K. Rimer, and K. Viswanath, eds., *Health behavior and health education: Theory, research and practice.* San Francisco: Jossey-Bassan, pp. 465–486.

Sport England, 2004. *The framework for sport in England.* London: Sport England.

Sport England, 2008. *Sport England strategy 2008–11.* London: Sport England.

Sport England, 2016. *Sport England: Towards an active nation, strategy 2016–2021.* London: Sport England.

Stuij, M., 2015. Habitus and social class: A case study on socialisation into sports and exercise. *Sport, Education and Society,* 20(6), pp. 780–798. http://dx.doi.org/10.1080/13573322.2013.827568

Tay, L. and Diener, E., 2011. Needs and subjective well-being around the world. *Journal of Personality and Social Psychology,* 101(2), pp. 354–365. http://dx.doi.org/10.1037/a0023779

Tinning, R., 2008. Pedagogy, sport pedagogy, and the field of kinesiology. *Quest,* 60(3), pp. 405–424.

UK Sport, 1999. *COMPASS: Sport participation in Europe.* London: UK Sport.

Van Bottenburg, M. and De Bosscher, V., 2011. An assessment of the impact of sports development on sports participation. In: B. Houlihan and M. Green, eds. *Routledge handbook of sports development.* London: Routledge. pp. 599–614

Van Bottenburg, M., Rijnen, B. and Sterkenburg, J. van, 2005. *Sports participation in the European Union: Trends and differences.* Nieuwegein, Netherlands: ARKO Sports Media.

Wankel, L. M., 1993. The importance of enjoyment to adherence and psychological benefits from physical activity. *International Journal of Sport Psychology*, 24(2), pp. 151–169.

Wankel, L. M. and Kreisel, P. S. J., 1985. Factors underlying enjoyment of youth sports: Sport and age group comparisons. *Journal of Sport Psychology*, 7(1), pp. 51–64.

Weinberg, R. S. and Gould, D., 2015. *Foundations of sport and exercise psychology*. 6th ed. Champagne, IL: Human Kinetics.

Chapter 2

The public policy challenge for community sport

The need for a theoretically driven paradigm shift

I started this book by saying that it is about an idea, the idea of 'sporting capital'. But the idea is the response to what appears to be a simple question, "why is it that some people become committed lifelong sport participants while others drop out from sport in their teens never to return to an active lifestyle?" (Rowe, 2015, p. 43). Like all questions of its type, it is simple to ask but very difficult to answer and even more difficult to find a 'solution' when a solution is defined in terms of preventing drop out, an outcome that is considered to be sufficiently in the public interest (in National Lottery terms defined as a 'good cause') to justify significant levels of public funding. Everyone involved in sports development knows that, like any other area of public policy intervention directed at social and behavioural change, there is no one 'silver bullet' that is the solution to an apparently simple question and there never will be just one. My response to this question is sophisticated and nuanced and is informed by the view, developed over many years at the forefront of sport policy and research and explored more fully in Chapter 4, that there has been a 'theoretical void' at the heart of sports development policy and practice that has served to undermine its impact and its justification. My central contention is that filling this void in the form of a coherent and robust theoretical foundation is "not just a nice to have discourse for academic debate but a fundamental pre-requisite for effective public policy" (Rowe, 2015, p. 43).

The public policy challenge for sport

I understand that to some a focus on theory may be seen as an academic distraction from the practical day-to-day business of how to get more people to take part in sport and create a 'sporting habit for life' (DCMS, 2012). My aim is to demonstrate an alternative view by making what I hope is a compelling argument supported by empirical evidence for a new theoretical foundation, the theory of sporting capital, that can drive a paradigm shift in sports development policy and practice to transform population wide levels of engagement in sport in England and contribute to a wider international debate. But some might say 'if it ain't broke don't fix it'. My starting point in making this argument is to focus attention in this chapter on a brief exploration of the success or otherwise of public policy in achieving its national aspirations for sport in England; what I have called 'the public policy challenge'. This challenge is not one that I have set personally but is one that successive Governments in the UK have subscribed to over many years. My argument is not to say that sport development has not had some successes. However, it is my contention that where these have occurred they have invariably been limited in reach, temporally constrained, localised, driven by charismatic individuals more so than nationally scalable intervention and poorly evidenced or understood in terms of mechanism, process and relationship to outcomes (on the latter point see for example Weiss,1993; Coalter, 2007). I would go so far as to contend that sports development as an emergent profession has lost ground and leverage because of its patent failure over more than 40 years to 'shift the curve' of participation at a national level or to narrow the structural demographic inequities particularly as they relate to gender, age and social class (Rowe and Moore, 2001; Rowe, 2002, 2004; Sport England, 1999; Sport England, 2000). My frustration has been enhanced by what I would characterise as a 'shopping list' approach to public policy programme design and intervention, often driven more by fashion and political imperative or motivation than by critical debate supported by evaluative evidence tempered by realistic ambitions. At its worst national public policy intervention has taken the form of a relentless recycling or reformulation of old ideas dressed up in new clothing supported by the linguistic devices of the day to give them an appearance of modernity and novelty.

The reality is that the early drop out from sport is an ongoing public policy concern that has shown few signs of transformational change since first identified as the 'Wolfenden Gap' over 50 years ago (Central Council of Physical Recreation (CCPR), (CCPR, 1960). If anything, the concerns have heightened as the drop out from sport has been accompanied by a more generalised shift into inactivity and its associated negative outcomes of increased obesity and poor health (Cavill, Kahlmeier and Racioppi, 2006; Department of Health, 2011; Public Health England, 2014). The concerns about stagnating or declining participation amongst the young have remained in the policy forefront in England. As recently as 2012 the then Government Sport Strategy, 'Creating a Sporting Habit for Life' (DCMS, 2012, p. 3) stated,

> This new Youth Sport Strategy aims to increase consistently the number of young people developing sport as a habit for life. Over the next five years, Sport England will invest at least £1 billion of Lottery and Exchequer funding to help to ensure that young people are regularly playing

sport and to break down the barriers that, until now, have prevented young people from continuing their interest in sport into their adult life.

The strategic focus on young people has since been reinforced in the most recent incarnation of Government Strategy (H. M. Government, 2015, p. 10) where the Sports Minister in the foreword states,

> Because we want everyone to get the best possible experience of sport from the earliest possible age, we are broadening Sport England's remit so that it becomes responsible for sport outside school from the age of five, rather than 14. A person's attitude towards sport is often shaped by their experience – or lack of experience – as a child, and many people drop out of sport before they even reach the age of 14. Getting Sport England involved earlier will help to combat this.

The broader concerns about stagnating participation in sport pre-date these recent Government pronouncements as reflected in a series of articles that Sport England published in April 2004 under the umbrella title 'Driving up participation: the challenge for sport' (Rowe, 2004, p. 2). In the editorial foreword to that publication I made the following observation,

> The situation in which we find ourselves is that participation rates have remained stubbornly static and inequities in participation between different social groups have continued largely unchanged over the last 30 years or so with perhaps the exception of more women taking part in fitness related activities. There are significant and growing numbers of people who live their lives in sedentary ways that were unheard of in previous generations.

Houlihan and White (2002, p. 21) argue that the significant public investment in the facility infrastructure for sport, particularly in the form of multi-sport leisure centres and swimming pools, during the 1970s and early 1980s "was to transform the opportunities for participating in sport". They go on to conclude that this investment released an expression of 'latent demand' but that by the 1980s there were clear signs of a policy shift away from facility provision to a strategy of concentrating resources on particular sports or sections of the community. This often took the form of investment in people including outreach work in the 'Action Sport' programme and more generally in the newly emergent sports development profession that followed. More recently Weed (2016, p. 569) has expressed a similar view,

> it appears that between 1977 and 1990 a range of provision focused sport participation policies catered for a level of unsatisfied latent demand for sport participation among those interested in sport by

making available a greater supply of sport facilities and removing structural barriers to the use of those facilities to create effective demand.

A belief in the potential to unlock latent demand in the context of the
stimulating effect anticipated for the Olympic and Paralympic Games was
discussed by Bullough (2012), but it was tempered by a cautious dose of
realism which has proved to be prescient given the continued 'flatlining' of
participation post the Games referred to later in this chapter. Grix and
Carmichael (2012) in their article unpacking the discourse around the justification for Government investment in elite sport raised a number of challenging questions prior to the London Olympic Games on the rationale and
evidence base for a 'virtuous cycle of sport' that automatically links elite
success to increased participation to wider health outcomes to an increase
in the 'talent pool' which in turn fuels increased elite success.

In 1995 the biggest annual national injection of funding for community
sport in England took place with the advent of the National Lottery and
the status afforded to sport as a good cause. Since 1995 Sport England
has invested £4.194 billion into 31,781 projects ranging from large multi-
sport facilities to sports clubs and revenue-based schemes (DCMS, 2016).
However, the impact of public policy intervention since the early 1990s has
been contentious. Rowe, Adams and Beasley, writing in 2004, summarised
evidence of trends in sports participation in the 1990s as pointing,

> towards broadly static levels of participation. . . . In addition although
> there is some evidence that some small progress has been made to nar-
> row 'the gender gap' there is no evidence to suggest that sport has wid-
> ened its participation base to include more people from low incomes,
> from different ethnic minorities and from people with a disability. This
> despite the many years of public policy priority focused on promoting
> 'sport for all' and extending participation amongst a range of 'targeted
> social groups'.
>
> (Rowe, 2004, p. 8)

Weed (2016, p. 569) in a critical review of the impact of sport policy
intervention on physical activity and health presents a synthesis of data
from a range of national surveys that

> show continuous growth in sport participation between 1977 and 1991
> totalling an additional 11% of the population, followed by a 2% fall
> between 1992 and 1997, a period of stagnation between 1998 and 2012
> (0.5% fall), and a further fall of 2% between 2012 and 2015.

In its own wide ranging review carried out in 2002 the Government
report, 'Game Plan' (DCMS and Strategy Unit, 2002) drawing on evidence

from the COMPASS Study (UK Sport, 1999), bemoaned the UK's low participation rates in sport when compared with Scandinavian countries. However, Van Bottenburg and De Bosscher (2011, p. 600), looking at the wider European perspective commented on the convergence of trends,

> Over the longer term, Western countries show a remarkable similarity in their sports participation trends. With some simplification, this trend can be characterized by an S-shaped curve: after a long initial period of slow but steady growth in sports participation from the introduction of modern sports until the middle of the twentieth century, nearly all Western countries experienced a massive increase in sports participation between the 1960s and 1980s. This was followed by a period of partial and temporary stagnation and, with respect to some age groups in some countries, even a slight decline in the 1990s, but overall and in the longer term sports participation continued to grow, albeit moderately.

The latest Eurobarometer sport participation survey across 28 member states of the European Union (Eurostat, 2014, p. 4) reported that,

> 41% of Europeans exercise or play sport at least once a week, while an important proportion of EU citizens (59%) never or seldom do so. The figures have not changed substantially since 2009. However, the proportion that never exercises or plays sport has increased from 39% to 42%.

Focusing on the structure of participation across different population subgroups Van Bottenburg, Rijnen and van Sterkenburg (2005, p. 37) concluded that,

> Sport is socially structured. In all EU member states, and thus throughout the entire European Union also, the degree of participation in sport differs between social population categories such as gender, age, level of education, profession and income. Despite the popularisation and democratisation of sport, it appears that these differences have continued to remain very persistent. They have diminished somewhat, but have not disappeared entirely, with the exception of some differences between men and women.

Coalter (2013, p. 12) cites research in the UK from 1995 (Coalter, Dowers and Baxter, 1995) which concluded that, "those staying in education after the minimal school leaving age were more likely to take part in sport and also to stay longer than those who left at the minimum age" and that "educational status explained a higher level of variance in participation across a broader range of sports than social class." Van Tuyckom, Scheerder and

Bracke (2010, p. 1081) in a review of sport participation statistics in 25 European countries came to the view that,

> Although no uniform conclusions can be drawn regarding the relationship between gender, age, and sports participation, the results nevertheless suggest that in some European countries, (which includes amongst the young in the UK) the traditional male domination of sport is still deeply rooted, whereas in others (Scandinavian countries and the Netherlands) it seems to be something of the past.

Writing in 2002 Scheerder et al. (p. 232) – drawing on the results of a statistical analysis of sport survey data in the Flanders dating back to 1969 – concluded that,

> Despite 25 years of the Sport for All movement, sharp contrasts still exist in sports involvement. At the end of the 20th century active involvement in sports is still related to social position and social class. The democratization of sports practices is not yet realized.

More recently Scheerder et al. (2011, p. 74), taking a European-wide perspective across 27 EU countries, came to very similar, if somewhat dispiriting conclusions, as Rowe did in his focus on England in 2004,

> despite all the aspirations and policy targets in the last decades equal levels of sports participation between social groups still seems out of reach. Social differences in sports participation are stronger than assumed and for all countries it holds true that sport participation is still socially stratified. Governments have not been able to solve these differences over time and therefore it remains a challenging prospect to truly achieve the Sport for All objectives.

Analysis of recent statistics from Sport England's Active People Survey (Sport England, 2013) presented in Figures 2.1 and 2.2 demonstrate the ongoing challenge. The 'flatlining' of overall rates of participation, the continuing 'participation gap' between the young and old, men and women and the lower and upper social class groups is clearly evident (see also Rowe, 2009). Experience in Canada indicates that,

> The national participation rates for Canadians age 15 years and older have been declining since 1992, and the participation rates for young Canadian adults are declining at a faster rate than that of older Canadians. In 2010, 26% of Canadians regularly participated in sport, which represents a decline of 17% since 1992.
>
> (Wood and Danylchuk, 2015, p. 157)

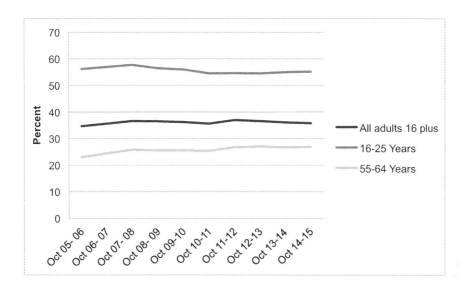

Figure 2.1 Changes in participation rates in sport in England overall and by age 2005/6 to 2014/15 (participation defined as at least once a week of 30 plus minutes' duration moderate intensity sport)

Source: Sport England Active People Survey (access: http://activepeople.sportengland.org/Result# ViewStateId=185&OutputType=2)

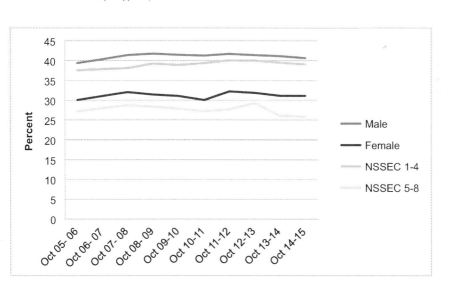

Figure 2.2 Changes in participation rates in sport in England by gender and social class 2005/6 to 2014/15 (participation defined as at least once a week of 30 plus minutes' duration moderate intensity sport)

Source: Sport England Active People Survey (access: http://activepeople.sportengland.org/Result# ViewStateId=185&OutputType=2)

This shows that the challenges are not confined to Europe but extend to other post industrialised countries. Nicholson, Hoye and Houlihan (2011, p. 305) examining sports participation polices and experience worldwide draw similar conclusions,

> It is evident . . . that government policies designed to increase sports participation have had limited success. . . . Some have had success . . . within small communities or specific cohorts . . . [but] the same level of success has not been apparent within the mass population.

The empirical trends in participation have contextualised but not, it appears, dented the aspirations of political administrations of left or right leaning persuasions or national sport agencies for setting what many would consider, certainly in hindsight and a view expressed by many commentators at the time, unrealistic goals for increasing levels of participation in sport (Collins, 2010; Coalter, 2013; Weed et al., 2015; Bullough, 2012; Houlihan, 2011). Recent and notable examples of this bullish approach are the Government's '70 percent target by 2020' (moving from 30 percent) in Game Plan (DCMS and Strategy Unit, 2002) to achieve what were estimated as comparable levels of participation to those found in Finland; and the Olympic legacy target of '1m people doing more sport by 2012–13' set by Government (DCMS, 2008) and Sport England (2008). It has now been accepted that both of these targets have or will be missed by a large margin and some have suggested that they have quietly been dropped (Weed, 2013; see also Bretherton, Piggin and Bodet, 2016) by Government and its arms' length body Sport England as they move on to new less easily quantified aspirations in their recently published strategy documents (H. M. Government, 2015; Sport England, 2016)

In some senses these failures to shift in any significant way national levels of participation in sport and associated structural inequalities over the last three decades could be justified, or at least explained, when the sociocultural context impacting on participation is considered. Sport England in its own strategy document 'The Framework for Sport in England' (Sport England, 2004) acknowledged the challenges associated with 'the key drivers of change' including an ageing population; increasing time pressures; increasing levels of overweight and obesity; and the growing disparity between the richest and poorest sections of society – all of which were more likely to drive rates of participation down than to increase them (see also Curry and Stanier, 2003). Coalter (2013, p. 18) has taken this argument further by suggesting the "possibility that the achievement of substantially higher participation rates is well beyond the control of sports policy" and that "in a sense sport is epiphenomenal, a secondary set of social practices dependent on and reflecting more fundamental structures, values and processes." He contemplates, drawing on the work of Wilson and Pickett

(2009), the possibility that given the high levels of inequality in the UK, and when compared to Scandinavian countries which set high benchmarks for the levels of participation in sport (Gratton, Rowe and Veal, 2011), it may be over-achieving.

The need for a paradigm shift: establishing a stronger theoretical foundation for community sports development

Although I would share Coalter's contention that sport is more framed by than impacting on inequality and other social processes, I have, as demonstrated in my earlier opening comments, an optimistic view that public policy intervention can be a positive catalyst for population wide behavioural change, albeit this is a view expressed with due caution and a number of caveats which we will come onto later. As already demonstrated, I also share Coalter's perspective (Coalter, 2007) that a stronger theoretical foundation is required if public policy is to have any chance of success in the face of what might be termed a set of 'wicked problems' (Rittel and Webber, 1973). Coalter (2007) identifies the need to go beyond necessary (participation) to achieve sufficient conditions and associated mechanisms if sport participation is to have any chance of achieving wider social outcomes (sport for development). Sporting capital theory takes an even more fundamental position viewing sustained participation as the behavioural outcome with sporting capital as the necessary conditions to deliver on that outcome. The important distinction is that participation in sport per se does not promote sustained participation, only a positive experience of participation that is matched with the psychological, physiological and social needs of the individual, i.e. that builds their levels of sporting capital, can deliver this outcome. The logic of the argument rehearsed earlier but worth repeating is that: 1) increased sporting capital leads to a higher probability of sustained participation in sport; and 2) increased sustained participation in sport under the right conditions can *potentially* lead to improved social, health and economic outcomes.

It is important at this stage to summarise and marshal my arguments to build a bridge to the next chapter which introduces and explains the theory of sporting capital. These arguments may be articulated as follows:

• There has been a nationally co-ordinated public policy commitment in the United Kingdom to increase participation in sport since the early 1970s. The evidence suggests, however, that in the 40-plus years that Governments (of all political persuasions) have had this policy commitment little has been achieved at least in a quantitative sense. Participation rates have remained broadly static over this period and in recent years may even have declined. Despite policy priorities focused on widening access, inequities in the social structure of participation in sport have changed very little. The higher socio-economic groups are still over three times more likely to participate than the lower socio-economic groups; boys and men continue to take part at significantly higher levels than girls and women (although public policy can claim some success in narrowing this gap) and participation rates continue to decline rapidly with age.

- This lack of quantifiable success has occurred despite significant (and perhaps never to be repeated) levels of public investment into community sport over this period. During the 1970s local authorities invested unprecedented amounts of money into indoor multi-purpose sports facilities to change the face of the sporting infrastructure across the country. The 1980s saw a huge commitment of investment into 'people' with the establishment of sport and leisure departments in local authorities and of the new 'sports development profession' (with significant financial support from the national Sports Councils). And since 1995 funding from the National Lottery has invested over £4 billion into community sport in England and London has hosted the Olympic and Paralympic Games with its promise of participation legacy that would impact on a generation.

- We must, however, not dismiss out of hand the achievements that have been made from public investment into sport over the last 40-plus years. This investment has undoubtedly improved the quality of participation for those who choose to participate. The minority who have regularly used local authority sports facilities over the years have clearly benefited from the experience; those who are members of sports clubs that for example have received lottery funding to extend or upgrade their facilities have been beneficiaries. However, improving the quality of participation for a minority in the population who already participate in organised sport has not been the stated principal aim of public policy objectives. Of even more concern is the suggestion that public investment in sport over this period has been regressive, tending to subsidise those who can afford to pay and not those who cannot and who have contributed disproportionately to income from lottery sales. There is also an argument that public subsidies have distorted the market in ways that it is difficult to assess. For example in the absence of public sector investment in health and fitness facilities would demand have been sufficient to have stimulated even greater private sector investment? Although the counter argument is that the relatively profitable health and fitness market has helped to cross subsidise less profitable areas of sport investment made by local authorities. Nevertheless it is difficult to come to any conclusion other than that public investment has very probably made sport better for the relatively advantaged 'sporting haves' whilst failing to make significant inroads into encouraging participation by the 'sporting have-nots'.

- The simple conclusion, and it is one that the Henley Centre also came to in their work on The Framework for Sport in England (Curry and Stanier, 2003) is that if we are to have any chance of achieving significant increases in participation we must do something different to what we have done over the last 30 to 40 years. The tantalising question remains, what is there different that we can do? The less palatable conclusion and the one suggested by Coalter (2013) is that we may be seeking to achieve the unachievable. Let us explore this further.

- It is impossible to say with certainty that significant and rapid increases in participation is achievable through public policy intervention. All we can seek to do is maximise the probability for achieving success. It is my contention that our chances of success will be optimised by designing public policy interventions that have a more sophisticated understanding of the triggers for stimulating behaviour change and the reinforcing mechanisms that will sustain participation, i.e. by building sporting capital. It is important to remember that there are very few if any people who have never participated in sport and that everyone has some level of sporting capital no matter how small. To this extent all those who currently do not participate, at least of say seven years of age and above, and even at this age we may consider active play as an antecedent to sports participation, have dropped out or lapsed. The challenge faced by public policy is to reduce the drop out in the first place and when lapses in participation take place, as they inevitably will, to get people back into sport as quickly as possible.

- It is clear from past experience what will not succeed. Public policy has arguably been characterised by a 'shopping list' mentality with a succession of programmes and initiatives that have little if any sound theoretical thinking or evidence base to support them. Anecdotal evidence, a contradiction in terms, has characterised and framed sports development policy and practice. The biggest failing has been to approach sports development with a limited understanding or perspective of the business it is in, that is the business of behaviour change and behaviour maintenance. Public policy statements and government strategies for sport have made little if any reference to the theoretical basis underpinning any of their recommendations. They have had no clear perspective on sports development as a dimension of behaviour change and have invariably been based on heroic untested assumptions often poorly articulated that if you do one thing it will inevitably and unquestionably lead to another thing. Build a sports centre in a deprived area and more people from deprived groups will participate. Design a marketing campaign that asks 'have you ever thought of sport?' and more people will think of sport and then having thought will start doing sport. Provide for more time for PE and competitive sport in the curriculum and more young people will leave school a lifelong sports participant.

Improve the information available to young people about sports clubs near where they live and make these clubs more young people friendly and more young people will join sports clubs when they leave school. Hold a major international sport event and people having watched it on television will be inspired to take part themselves. Sport England's current strategy (Sport England, 2016) has gone some way to addressing this theoretical void by making reference to the transtheoretical model of behaviour change drawn from a health and physical activity paradigm. But this link is arguably limited, drawn from a medically dominated model of health and lifestyle related behaviours and has yet to be demonstrated as an integral and effective theoretical underpinning appropriate to the context of sport (see Chapter 4).

- How can we increase participation in sport poses a simple question. But, as with most areas of public policy, it is a simple question with no one simple answer. There is no 'silver bullet', no clear and simple strategy with straightforward and predictable outcomes, no clear direction that says 'if you do a) then b) will follow'. This is hardly surprising when we are talking about lifestyle-related behaviour change across a whole population. In pursuit of these outcomes, which are considered to be in the public interest, we are confronted with multiple factors that impact on the decision 'to be a sports participant' or 'not to be a sports participant'. Sport policy and practice operates in the world of 'wicked problems' where uncertainty, complexity, power relations, value systems and unintended consequences are the norm not the exception. "You don't so much "solve" a wicked problem as you help stakeholders negotiate shared understanding and shared meaning about the problem and its possible solutions" (Conklin, Basadur and Van Patter, 2007, p. 3).

- Although biology and genetic factors will have a bearing on the potential to be a high performer in sport, it is safe to say that there is little in people's biological make-up that would determine from birth whether someone in later life will become a sedentary person while another becomes a very active one. It may in fact be posited that being active has in evolutionary terms been a favourable factor in the 'survival of the fittest' and that it is only over very recent times in terms of human evolutionary development that the environments in which we live and reward systems in which we operate have begun to make inactivity less important as a survival factor. Although there appear to be few 'social penalties' for being inactive, we are increasingly seeing the 'biological penalties' in what has been termed by some commentators an obesity epidemic associated in turn with startling increases in late onset diabetes, now nowhere near as 'late' as it used to be, and early onset osteoporosis just to mention two health conditions associated with sedentary behaviours.

- The fact that we do not have biology working against us, in fact it is working for us as the consequences of chronic inactivity become more and more visible and hence difficult to banish to the back of our collective consciences, is a big plus factor. It at least gives us a fighting chance to turn behaviour around. If biology is not the primary factor, then what is? It is not possible to isolate one primary factor, but there is a sound theoretical base with some supporting evidence to suggest what the ingredients are that differentiate a participant from a non participant. Whether someone participates in sport or does not participate in sport is influenced by their physical competence, the skills necessary to participate at a level that is enjoyable; their own value system that shapes their personal identities, beliefs and attitudes; and their social networks, the people around them particularly their family, and their peer group (see the evidence in Chapter 5). In turn these individual value systems and characteristics are mediated by the socio-cultural and physical environment in which people live which either enable and reinforce participation or militate against or operates as a disincentive to it.

It is now time to provide my response to these issues by introducing the theory of sporting capital, its component parts and central propositions and to highlight some of the public policy implications that flow from it.

References

Bretherton, P., Piggin, J. and Bodet, G., 2016. Olympic sport and physical activity promotion: The rise and fall of the London 2012 pre-event mass participation 'legacy'. *International Journal of Sport Policy and Politics*, 8(4), pp. 609–624. http://dx.doi.org/10.1080/19406940.2016.1229686

Bullough, S. J., 2012. A new look at the latent demand for sport and its potential to deliver a positive legacy for London 2012. *International Journal of Sport Policy and Politics*, 4(1), pp. 39–54. http://dx.doi.org/10.1080/19406940.2011.627357

Cavill, N., Kahlmeier, S. and Racioppi, F., 2006. *Physical activity and health in Europe: Evidence for action*. Copenhagen: World Health Organisation.

Central Council of Physical Recreation Great Britain, 1960. *Sport & the community: The report of the Wolfenden Committee on Sport* (Chairman, Sir John Wolfenden). London: HMSO.

Coalter, F., 2007. *A wider social role for sport: Who's keeping the score*. London: Routledge.

Coalter, F., 2013. Game plan and the spirit level: The class ceiling and the limits of sports policy? *International Journal of Sport Policy and Politics*, 5(1), pp. 3–19. http://dx.doi.org/10.1080/19406940.2012.656690

Coalter, F., Dowers, S. and Baxter, M., 1995. The impact of social class and education on sports participation: Some evidence from the general household survey. In: K. Roberts, ed. *Leisure and social stratification*. Brighton: Leisure Studies Association.

Collins, M., 2010. From 'sport for good' to 'sport for sport's sake' – not a good move for sports development in England? *International Journal of Sport Policy*, 2(3), pp. 367–379.

Conklin, J., Basadur, M. and Van Patter, G., 2007. Rethinking wicked problems: Unpacking paradigms, bridging universes: Interview. *NextD Journal*, (10), pp. 1–30, Conversation 10.1.

Curry, A. and Stanier, R., 2003. *Strategic framework for community sport in England: Meeting the challenge of game plan: Emerging insights on the future of participation in sport in England*. An Interim Report to Sport England. Reading: The Henley Centre.

Department for Culture, Media and Sport, 2008. *Before, during and after: Making the most of the London 2012 Games*. London: DCMS.

Department for Culture, Media and Sport, 2012. *Creating a sporting habit for life: A new youth sport strategy*. London: DCMS.

Department for Culture, Media and Sport, 2016. *National lottery grants search: Grants awarded by distributing body* [online]. Available at: <www.lottery.culture. gov.uk/GrantsByDistributingBody.aspx> [accessed 6th December 2016].

Department for Culture, Media and Sport and the Strategy Unit, 2002. *Game plan: A strategy for delivering government's sport and physical activity objectives*. London: Cabinet Office.

Department of Health, 2011. *Start active, stay active: A report on physical activity from the four home countries' Chief Medical Officers*. London: The Stationery Office Limited.

Eurostat, 2014. *Sport and physical activity report*. Special Eurobarometer 412. Brussels: European Commission.

Gratton, C., Rowe, N. and Veal, A. J., 2011. International Comparisons of Sports participation in European Countries: an Update of the COMPASS Project. *European Journal for Sport and Society*, 8(1/2), pp 99–116

Grix, J. and Carmichael, F., 2012. Why do governments invest in elite sport? A polemic. *International Journal of Sport Policy and Politics*, 4(1), pp. 73–90.

H. M. Government, 2015. *Sporting future: A new strategy for an active nation*. London: Cabinet Office.

Houlihan, B., 2011. England. In: M. Nicholson, H. Hoye, and B. Houlihan, eds. *Participation in sport, international policy perspectives*. London: Routledge, pp. 10–24.

Houlihan, B. and White, A., 2002. *The politics of sport development: Development of sport or development through sport?* London: Routledge.

Nicholson, M., Hoye, R. and Houlihan, B. eds., 2011. *Participation in sport: International perspectives*. London: Routledge.

Public Health England, 2014. *Everybody active, every day: An evidence-based approach to physical activity*. London: Public Health England.

Rittel, H. W. J. and Webber, M. M., 1973. Dilemmas in a general theory of planning. *Policy Sciences*, 4(2), pp. 155–169.

Rowe, N. F., 2002. *Sports equity index for regular participation*. London: Sport England.

Rowe, N. F. ed., 2004. *Driving up participation: The challenge for sport*. London: Sport England.

Rowe, N. F., 2009. The active people survey: A catalyst for transforming evidence-based sport policy in England. *International Journal of Sport Policy and Politics*, 1(1), pp. 89–98. http://dx.doi.org/10.1080/19406940802681244

Rowe, N. F., 2015. Sporting capital: A theoretical and empirical analysis of sport participation determinants and its application to sports development policy and practice. *International Journal of Sport Policy and Politics*, 7(1), pp. 43–61.

Rowe, N. F., Adams, R. and Beasley, N., 2004. Driving up participation in sport: The social context, the trends, the prospects and the challenges. In: N. F. Rowe, ed. *Driving up participation: The challenge for sport*. London: Sport England, pp. 6–13.

Rowe, N. F. and Moore, S., 2001. *Participation in sport: Past trends and future prospects*. London: UK Sport and Sport England.

Scheerder, J., Vandermeerschen, H., Van Tuyckom, C., Hoekman, R., Breedveld, K. and Vos, S., 2011. *Understanding the game, sport participation in Europe, facts, reflections and recommendations*. Sport Policy and Management Report 10. Leuven, Belgium: Research Unit of Social Kinesiology and Sport Management of the K. U. Leuven.

Scheerder, J., Vanreusel, B., Taks, M. and Renson, R., 2002. Social sports stratification in Flanders 1969–1999: Intergenerational reproduction of social inequalities? *International Review for the Sociology of Sport*, 37(2), pp. 219–245. http://dx.doi.org/10.1177/1012690202037002006.

Sport England, 1999. *Survey of sports halls and swimming pools in England*. London: Sport England.

Sport England, 2000. *Performance measurement for local authority sports halls and swimming pools*. London: Sport England.

Sport England, 2004. *The framework for sport in England*. London: Sport England.

Sport England, 2008. *Sport England strategy 2008–11*. London: Sport England.

Sport England, 2013. *Active people interactive* [online]. Available at: <http://active-people.sportengland.org> [accessed 13th December 2016].

Sport England, 2016. *Sport England: Towards an active nation, strategy 2016–2021*. London: Sport England.

UK Sport, 1999. *COMPASS: Sport participation in Europe*. London: UK Sport.

Van Bottenburg, M. and De Bosscher, V., 2011. An assessment of the impact of sports development on sports participation. In: B. Houlihan and M. Green, eds. *Routledge handbook of sports development*. London: Routledge. pp. 599–614.

Van Bottenburg, M., Rijnen, B. and Sterkenburg, J. van, 2005. *Sports participation in the European Union: Trends and differences*. Nieuwegein, Netherlands: Arko Sports Media.

Van Tuyckom, C., Scheerder, J. and Bracke, P., 2010. Gender and age inequalities in regular sports participation: A crossnational study of 25 European countries. *Journal of Sports Sciences*, 28(10), pp. 1077–1084. http://dx.doi.org/10.1080/02640414.2010.492229

Weed, M., 2013. London 2012 legacy strategy: Ambitions, promises and implementation plans. In: V. Girginov, ed. *Handbook of the London 2012 Olympic and Paralympic Games* (Volume One). Great Britain: Routledge, pp. 87–98.

Weed, M., 2016. Should we privilege sport for health? The comparative effectiveness of UK government investment in sport as a public health intervention. *International Journal of Sport Policy and Politics*, 8(4), pp. 559–576.

Weed, M., Coren, E., Fiore, J., Wellard, I., Chatziefstathiou, D., Mansfield, L. and Dowse, S., 2015. The Olympic Games and raising sport participation: A systematic review of evidence and an interrogation of policy for a demonstration effect. *European Sport Management Quarterly*, 15(2), pp. 195–226. http://dx.doi.org/1 0.1080/16184742.2014.998695

Weiss, C. H., 1993. Where politics and evaluation research meet. *Evaluation Practice*, 14(1), pp. 93–106.

Wilson, R. and Pickett, K., 2009. *The spirit level: Why more equal societies almost always do better*. London: Allen Lane.

Wood, L. and Danylchuk, K., 2015. The impact of constraints and negotiation strategies on involvement in intramural sport. *Managing Sport & Leisure*, 20(3), pp. 157–173.

Sporting capital – what is it, how does it relate to other forms of human, cultural and social capital and why is it important?

In this chapter I define 'sporting capital'; introduce its component parts; explore its relationships with other forms of 'capital'; articulate some of the propositions that flow from the theory; examine the relationship between sporting capital and external barriers and constraints; locate sporting capital in its broader socio-cultural context; and conclude by identifying the key links and implications for sports development policy and practice.

What is sporting capital?

Sport is a socio-cultural construct and any effective theory of sporting behaviour and its determinants must embed these aspects of the very nature of sport as an integral part of the theory. Sporting capital does this by addressing the particular and sport-specific factors that are influential in both the decision to participate in sport at any given time but also, importantly, the likelihood of sustaining that participation over time. Sporting capital is an integrated holistic theory that explains and provides insight into the reasons for participation and non participation in sport and the variations in participation across different sub-groups in the population (Rowe, 2015). As a theoretical construct it is most closely analogous to 'human capital'. It incorporates but is different to 'social capital' and has some similarities with but again is different to 'cultural capital'. To fully understand sporting capital it is important to spend some time examining these relationships and antecedents.

The theory of sporting capital is as far as the author can discern a new conceptualisation, albeit none of the component parts are new. If you google 'sporting capital' you will, at the time of writing, see items about Melbourne or London; sporting capital as a place. Stempel (2006) has referred to 'sporting capital' as an economic value associated with 'investment' in sport as a successful high school athlete leading to improved job and income prospects in later life, i.e. sport as a form of human capital. A study carried out in a rural setting in Victoria, Australia (Driscoll and Wood, 1999) refers to 'sporting capital' as an outcome generating increased social capital through the networks of volunteers and community clubs associated with sports provision in a community. Both of these studies have conceptualised sporting capital as contributing to an outcome, in these cases human or social capital, rather than, as proposed here, a theoretical construct in its own right, as an antecedent to and explanation of individual sporting behaviour and its change over time. An article published in 2015 by Stuij does use the term 'sporting capital' in a similar way as conceived here, making a link to cultural capital and to Bourdieu's concept of the habitus but does not go on to extend and develop these ideas into a holistic theoretical construct.

Sporting capital as conceived here is most closely related to the theory of 'human capital' which is an economic concept developed initially by Jacob Mincer and Gary Becker of the "Chicago School" of economics. Becker's book entitled 'Human Capital', published over half a century ago (Becker, 1964), became a standard reference for many years and continues to be of influence. Human capital may be defined as, "the stock of competencies, knowledge and personality attributes embodied in the ability to perform labour so as to produce economic value. It is the attributes gained by a worker through education and experience" (see Rowe, 2015, p. 47).

Human capital is the attributes a person has that are productive in some economic context. Economists regard expenditures on education, training, medical care, and so on as investments in human capital. It is called human capital because these qualities are attached and inseparable from the individual. People cannot be separated from their knowledge, skills, health, or values in the way they can be separated, for example, from other more tangible forms of capital such as their financial and physical assets. Important qualities associated with human capital are that it can appreciate or depreciate over time; elements of it are transferable between individuals; that it is durable and isn't diminished with use (in fact it increases with use); it can be increased both by education and by 'on the job experience'; it has both a micro dimension in relation to the link between children and their parents and a macro dimension in terms of its broader relationship to economic growth and the wealth of a nation (Rowe, 2015). Human capital derives partly from experiences gained in the household-of-origin, partly from participation in the educational system and finally from previous participation in paid work activities (Gershuny, 2003).

Similarly we would expect that sporting capital would be formed initially in the family; then through experience of PE in the school environment and for some into further and higher education; and progressively into and through adulthood to be shaped and influenced by one's peers and relationships and experiences in community settings of sports clubs, health and fitness facilities and informal recreational settings. As we will see later these characteristics of human capital translate directly into that of 'sporting capital' and are key aspects of the concept. So, drawing from the concept of human capital, sporting capital may be defined as: "the stock of physiological, sociological and psychological attributes and competencies that support and motivate an individual to participate in sport and to sustain that participation over time." (Rowe, 2015, p. 45)

Before elaborating further on the constituent 'domains' that make up sporting capital and its important characteristics, it is worthwhile clarifying its differences and relationship to both cultural capital and social capital.

How does sporting capital relate to other forms of human, cultural and social capital?

The term 'cultural capital' is a sociological concept that has received widespread popularity since it was first articulated by Pierre Bourdieu (1986). It refers to non-financial social assets that promote social mobility beyond economic means. Put another way, cultural capital consists of the knowledge, skills, education, and advantages that a person has which give them a higher status in society. For example parents provide their children with cultural capital by transmitting the attitudes and knowledge needed to succeed in the current educational system. Other examples of cultural capital include intellect, style of speech, dress and even physical appearance. Bourdieu (1986) identifies three variants of cultural capital: first, in the embodied state incorporated in mind and body (that is both the consciously acquired and passively inherited properties of oneself, acquired through a socialisation process usually within the family); second, in the institutionalised state, that is, in institutionalised forms such as educational qualifications; and third, in the objectified state, simply existing as cultural goods such as books, artefacts, dictionaries and paintings. Bourdieu referred to 'physical capital' under the heading of cultural capital. However, Shilling (1991, p. 654) contended that the "physical is too important to be seen merely as a subdivision of cultural capital". Shilling went on to argue that it is possible to view the body as possessing physical capital, encompassing body size, shape, physique, appearance and performance, the production of which refers to the ways bodies are afforded symbolic value in various social fields (Shilling, 1991). Warde (2006, p. 121) refers to the strong evidence of the development and legitimacy of a body maintenance culture and suggests that, "Not only through practices of sport and exercise, but also through diet and body management, modification and maintenance, do people introduce and represent themselves and their social strategies and values to others" and to "the exercised body as a 'component of social classification'". Sporting capital incorporates elements of cultural, social and physical capital that operates in the social field of sport with all its associated rules, regulations, conventions, social norms, gender and power relationships.

Bourdieu envisages a process by which one form of capital can be transformed or converted into another. For example, economic capital can be converted into cultural capital, while cultural capital can be readily translated into social capital. Shilling (1993) suggests that physical capital can be converted into economic capital (in the form of professional sports and sponsorship), cultural capital (in the form of scholarships to universities and enhanced education) and social capital (in the form of social networks and connections through sports organisations). This transformational nature or 'transferability of capitals' is an important concept when applied to sporting capital. It is easy to see when we explore them later that the attributes that make up sporting capital can also increase cultural capital through the status and social recognition that accompanies sporting achievement and the physical qualities associated with it. This does not mean, however, that sporting capital is the same thing as cultural capital and that acquiring sporting capital necessarily or automatically increases cultural capital or vice versa. See for example the evidence reviewed in Chapter 5 which suggests that peer pressure on young women can push them away from sport because of its low status amongst many in the dominant culture of this demographic. Similarly it is easy to envisage how sporting capital can be translated into human capital when professional 'athletes' make their living from their sporting prowess. Less clear or direct, but no less important from a societal perspective, is how participation in sport has the potential to build attributes such as team working, dedication, interpersonal skills and self discipline that translate into valued marketable qualities in the workplace, again sport as a means to increase human capital. Duckworth et al. (2007) refer to the importance of the quality of 'grit', i.e. persistence of effort in achieving long-term goals in life, a quality often associated with sporting achievements.

An interesting concept that Bourdieu raises that has relevance in its application to sporting capital is the 'domestic transmission of cultural capital.' He argues that "scholastic yield from educational action, that is levels of educational attainment, depends on the cultural capital previously invested by the family" (Bourdieu 1996. p. 244), i.e. the early socialisation process (Goldthorpe, undated; see also De Graaf, De Graaf and Kraaykamp, 2000). For Bourdieu this results in the reproduction of a 'dominant social class.' The parallels are interesting, raising the question of whether sporting capital is transmitted in similar ways to cultural capital through the slow but pervasive process of socialisation that happens in the family. If this is the case, we would expect to see a direct relationship between the levels of sporting capital of parents and their children and an ongoing challenge for the school environment and other 'post family' experiences to redress these differences (see Chapter 5). According to Goldthorpe (undated, p. 9-10) Bourdieu, in the case of cultural capital, only allowed in exceptional cases for the potential impact of the school and other educational institutions to "radically redress or 'make over' other forms of habitus that children may bring to them". However, Goldthorpe (undated, p. 13), reviewing evidence on the impact of education on social mobility in 1970s Britain, critiqued

Bourdieu's position, concluding that "the idea that the habitus, as initially formed by family and class, may be subject to confirmation by the school but not, other than exceptionally, to any kind of reconstitution is directly called into question." Goldthorpe quotes Halsey, Heath and Ridge (1980, p. 77), who concluded from evidence gathered in the 1970s that schools "were doing far more than 'reproducing' cultural capital; they were creating it, too". Extending the parallels, such a conclusion suggests a degree of optimism that schools can make a meaningful and significant impact on young people's levels of sporting capital no matter what advantage or disadvantage their family background confers. I return to explore these issues more fully in Chapters 5 and 8.

Sporting capital also has a close relationship to social capital, although the two should not be confused, conflated or used interchangeably. The discourse on social capital has been more prevalent in sport policy than have the concepts of cultural or human capital, stimulated as it was by the publication of Putnam's 'Bowling Alone' (Putnam, 2000). As Tlili and Obsiye (2014, p. 551) note, "the concept has 'not only been popular in academia, but has also become a buzzword among politicians and policymakers". In the same article they reference Coleman's observation that,

> [un]like other forms of capital, social capital inheres in the structure of relations between actors and among actors. . . . In other words, social capital is very social, very relational, unlike other forms of capital – notably economic capital – that can be abstracted from their social and interpersonal networks.
>
> (Tlili and Obsiye, p. 553)

Social capital may appear to be a straightforward concept about the social connectedness of individuals within a wider community, and as Nicholson and Hoye (2008, p. 3) contend, "there is an inherent logic in the idea that the more connections individuals make within their communities the better off they will be emotionally, socially, physically and economically". However, social capital is a slippery concept with many definitions and interpretations (see Coalter, 2007). Bourdieu (1986, p. 248) described social capital as, "the aggregate of the actual or potential resources which are linked to possession of a durable network of more or less institutionalized relationships of mutual acquaintance and recognition." In these terms social capital can bring economic advantage to the individual possessing it. Putnam (2000), on the other hand, extends social capital to embrace wider community relationships of trust, reciprocity and civic value and bemoans the decline of these values in American life.

Many commentators have stressed that social capital is not inherently good or bad although the term is more generally, in policy circles at least, associated with positive rather than negative outcomes. The distinction between 'bonding' (ties and interactions between like people) and 'bridg-ing' (the inter-group links that bring different types of people together) social capital is an important one elucidated eloquently by Putnam (2000, p. 23) as follows: "Bonding social capital constitutes a kind of sociological superglue, whereas bridging social capital provides a sociological WD-40". Social capital transmuted politically in what transpired to be the relatively short-lived enthusiasm by the Conservative Lib Dem Coalition Government for the idea of the 'Big Society' (The Cabinet Office, 2010), "based around encouraging greater personal and family responsibility and community activism" (BBC, 2010) i.e. social action encouraging and enabling people to play a more active part in society. The relationship of sport to social capital seems an obvious one. Engagement in sport including participating, spectating and volunteering, mostly takes place in social networks ranging, for example, from traditional voluntary sports clubs, to health and fitness classes to the less formalised social interactions associated with meeting people in local parks, using community sport facilities and attending sport-ing events (hence the reference to 'Bowling' in the title of Putnam's seminal publication). By definition, taking part in sport can build social capital, although, in academic circles at least, there is an ongoing debate as to the nature of that 'capital' (bonding or bridging), the balance between pro-social and potentially negative outcomes and the evidence supporting the more extensive claims made for sport in terms of promoting community cohesion, social inclusion and civic renewal (Coalter, 2007). The contribu-tors to Nicholson and Hoye's (2008) publication provide an extensive cri-tique and exploration of the relationship between sport and social capital. The important point to note here, however, is that like human and cultural capital, social capital is again a related but different concept to sporting capital. Increased sporting capital can lead to increased social capital and importantly, as we shall see later, the sport specific ingredients of social capital, 'social connectedness through sport' is not just a potential product of sporting capital but also an integral aspect or domain within it.

So to summarise – sporting capital may be defined as: *The stock of physi-ological, social and psychological attributes and competencies that support and motivate an individual to participate in sport and to sustain that par-ticipation over time*. It is a theory that can help us to better understand and explain sporting behaviour across individuals (micro), communities (meso) and populations (macro). The distinctions made between the different types of 'capital', human, cultural and social and the relationships between them help in turn to define and clarify what is meant by 'sporting capital'. However, the important points to take away from this section are as follows:

- Sporting capital is analogous to human capital and incorporates many of the same characteristics and qualities. It can be thought of as a 'stock' that an individual holds and that is inseparable from them.

- Sporting capital is related to human, cultural and social capital in subtle and different ways but it is not the same as these concepts. Importantly as a theoretical construct it can stand alone in its specificity and relevance to sports development policy and practice.
- Sporting capital has the potential to be transferred into and to build human, social and cultural capital and, in turn, increases in some aspects of these other 'capitals' can enhance and support increases in sporting capital.
- Social capital when defined in a narrow sense of an individual's 'social connections and networks in sport' is embedded as an integral part of the construction of sporting capital. In this context social capital is primarily seen as an input to and one of the determinant factors of sport participation rather than as an outcome from that participation.

What are the constituents of sporting capital, its characteristics and the implications for public policy and practice?

Having provided a broad definition of sporting capital and located it in relation to other forms of capital, I will now turn the focus towards exploring its constituent 'domains' and the theoretical propositions that flow from it (see also Rowe, 2015). Sporting capital theory proposes that the underlying factors that determine the likelihood of people participating in sport can be classified into three domains: social, psychological and physiological (which includes physical health and physical competency). Brought together, these three domains interact and combine to create an individual's overall level of 'sporting capital'. It is proposed that levels of sporting capital not only determine the likelihood of current participation but also impact on the probability that it will be sustained into later life. People with high levels of sporting capital are much more likely to engage in lifelong participation than their peers with low levels of sporting capital. Consequently, the theory suggests that an individual's level of sporting capital at any given point in time will provide a much better predictor of sustained future participation in sport than measuring the prevalence of current behaviour (sport participation) alone.

The model (Rowe, 2015) (see Figure 3.1) suggests a dynamic interaction between physiological, psychological and social factors, all of which play a significant role in determining current and likely future sports participation. The model predicts that an individual who scores positively on the three domains will have a high probability of current and future sustained participation, while someone who scores poorly will have a very low probability of both current and future sustained participation in sport.

In simple terms sporting capital may be thought of as the 'locked in potential' to participate in sport. It is the in-built capacities that make us feel

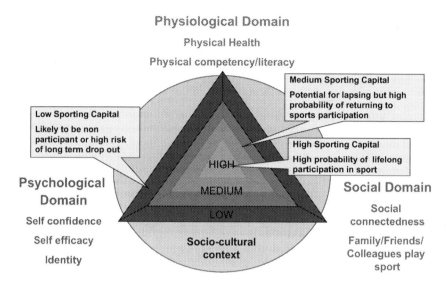

Figure 3.1 Model of sporting capital

good and confident about ourselves in sporty situations; confident that we can acquit ourselves without fear of embarrassment and without concerns over how we look; that we have the skills and competencies that enable us to enjoy and get better at sport; and that we have the friendship networks that support and nurture our continued participation. Everyone has sporting capital but for some the levels are so low, even at a very young age, that the desire and confidence to participate is not there and even where there is some motivation the barriers, no matter how small, seem insurmountable. Like human capital the 'stock' of sporting capital held by an individual is inseparable from them, can be increased with education and positive experiences and can be decreased by negative experiences and inactivity with attrition over time. Sporting capital is invisible until it is expressed through the act of taking part in sport when it becomes tangible. Although lacking a theoretical foundation, it is generally understood and appreciated in every-day contexts in terms of an individuals' sense of their own personal identity and their assessment of others. So, for example, we often hear expressions of someone being 'very sporty' or a 'sporty type of person' with the reasons for this often mistakenly attributed solely to 'natural' or inherent qualities rather than substantially a consequence of processes of socialisation and experience.

The theory of sporting capital would suggest that higher levels enhance an individuals' opportunity to gain enjoyment from participating in sport through the increased opportunity for self expression, control and mastery over a challenge that it brings. For some sports, and particularly the technically more challenging ones, a relatively high level of sporting capital is required to engage in the sport in what might be considered a meaningful way. Take for example two novice tennis players unable to sustain a rally, someone new to golf who is unable to get a ball airborne or a rugby player not prepared or able to engage in the requisite level of physicality. The concept of 'flow' has relevance here. Flow as a holistic construct is commonly defined by nine characteristics or dimensions (Csikszentmihalyi, 1990). Three of these dimensions, challenge-skill balance, clear proximal goals, and unambiguous feedback, are considered to be flow conditions. When fulfilled, these three flow conditions facilitate the subjective experience of being in a flow state. Generally flow results in heightened feelings of well-being (Csikszentmihalyi, 1978; Haworth, 1993 Nakamura and Csikszentmihalyi, 2005). Flow states are not just experienced in optimal elite sport environments. Jackson et al. (1998) found an association between flow and three psychological variables: intrinsic motivation (positive); perceived ability (positive); and cognitive anxiety (negative). Csikszentmihalyi (1990, p. 95) has gone so far as to suggest that within the flow model, "it is not the skills we actually have that determine how we feel but the ones we think we have." Csikszentmihalyi and Nakamura (1989) suggest that both challenges and skills must be relatively high before anything resembling a flow experience comes about. Flow is achieved when an individual has a sense that he or she is engaging in challenges that match or slightly exceed their capacities (in my terms their level of sporting capital). When the challenge is too high for the ability level (sporting capital), anxiety arises and where it is too low boredom. In both cases (over stimulation and under stimulation) the potential for drop out is enhanced. This 'matching' of design of the intervention to the level of sporting capital is something I return to in Chapter 8.

An individual's level of sporting capital is framed and shaped by the socio-cultural context in which they live. The debate about the relative balance of 'nurture' or 'nature' has less relevance when it comes to sporting capital than it may have for example in the context of elite level sport performance, and even here it is contentious (Bakera and Horton, 2004). Sporting capital is not synonymous with levels of sporting performance although the two are clearly related, and it would be difficult to envisage an elite level athlete who did not have exceptionally high levels of sporting capital. Although there will be a small genetic component, particularly as it relates to 'physicality', the level of sporting capital a person achieves and maintains in life is primarily a consequence of a socialisation process and the environment in which they live. This would suggest that sporting capital is not evenly distributed either geographically across local communities, regions and nations or amongst different sub-groups in the population.

The empirical evidence presented in Chapters 6 and 7 test this proposition. Although many individuals will have what might be considered a 'deficit' of sporting capital, i.e. less than the requisite level to sustain a high probability of participating in sport throughout the life-course, the responsibility for this deficit cannot be ascribed to the individual any more than, for example, the causes of poverty can be blamed on the poor.

Although sporting capital is a crucial determinant of participation, it is not the sole one. The theory proposes that higher levels of sporting capital will increase the likelihood of an individual participating by increasing the level of motivation, the desire to participate and the increased potential it provides for a positive experience associated with taking part, i.e. a positive feedback loop. However, for any given individual the decision to participate will be moderated by the opportunities available and the external barriers and constraints that impact on those opportunities whether personal – e.g. in the family, social – e.g. in the community, environmental – e.g. in terms of suitable places to play or economic in terms of affordability (see Chapter 5). Everything else being equal in terms of the opportunities available and the constraints and barriers faced, individuals with the same level of sporting capital will have the same probability of participating. However, differences in personal and local circumstances can impact on individuals with the same levels of sporting capital to give them different probabilities of participating in sport. Notwithstanding, with increasing levels of sporting capital comes increasing levels of resilience to the external constraints and barriers to participation.

The relationship between sporting capital and barriers and constraints to participation is a critical one. Although the theory of sporting capital is primarily concerned with individual capacity building and empowerment, i.e. 'demand creation', it incorporates within the theory the importance and impact of barriers and constraints to participation that are 'external' to the individual (see Crawford, Jackson and Godbey, 1991). External barriers or constraints operate to either prevent or mediate participant behaviour. They can be physical, economic or socio-cultural and are invariably characterised by a lack of control or influence, real or perceived, by the individual over the nature and extent of the barrier. Individuals' perception of leisure constraints is known to play an important role in the decision to quit or reduce participation in diverse activities (Crawford and Godbey, 1987). Reduction in barriers or constraints can operate positively to serve as a lever to increase participation. External barriers include, for example, those related to price, facility supply and quality, customer service, childcare and workplace opportunities. Leisure constraints are not viewed in most cases as insurmountable obstacles, but instead are seen as negotiable. Jackson, Crawford and Godbey (1993, p. 4) argue that participation, "is dependent not on the absence of constraints (although this may be true for some people) but on negotiation through them. Such negotiations may modify rather than foreclose participation." Sporting capital interacts with barriers and constraints in complex and subtle ways by influencing individual negotiation strategies in a positive way for people with high levels of sporting capital and negatively for those on low levels. So, for example, what might be an insurmountable barrier to participation for someone with low levels of sporting capital may be perceived as a small inconvenience to be overcome or not noticed at all by his or her contemporary with high levels. A classic example is the barrier of 'time pressure' which often emerges as the single biggest constraint in opinion and participation surveys (see for example Matthews et al., 2016; Eurostat, 2014). In modern lives time pressures do exist; however, for many, time pressure is more an expression of individual choice, priority and motivation than an objective reality (Gershuny, 2003). So a 'busy' individual with high levels of sporting capital is sufficiently motivated to 'make time for sport' whereas a less busy individual with low levels of sporting capital 'hasn't got the time to fit sport into their lives' (see Fisher, 2002 for evidence that the busiest individuals are the most physically active). Invariably it is not 'time' that is the critical variable but motivation which, I would contend, is underpinned by an individual's level of sporting capital.

Public policy intervention has historically been skewed towards barrier/ constraint reduction and 'opportunity creation' without due understanding and regard to its interaction with levels of sporting capital. It is the case that in some circumstances and for some people, in particular those non participants with moderate to high levels of sporting capital, external barrier/constraint reduction will provide good returns on investment by releasing 'latent demand'. However, for others in different contexts and with moderate to low levels of sporting capital, which includes many of the most sedentary and least healthy in society, barrier and constraint reduction in the absence of any intervention designed to build sporting capital will have limited impact and be of questionable value. But perhaps of even greater importance, the potential gains from what might be relatively modest increases in average levels of sporting capital across the population are significant and will be likely to outstrip anything that could be delivered by a predominant focus on barrier reduction alone.

This *theoretical relationship* between sporting capital levels and barrier reduction is demonstrated in Figure 3.2. The horizontal axis is a hypothetical scale of the barriers to participation with 1 being very low and 10 being very high. Imagine this scale to be a synthesis of all the external barriers an individual might face at any given time. The vertical axis is the probability of participating in sport. The plotted lines are three different levels of sporting capital: low (an index score of 1–4); medium (a score of 5–7); and high (a score of 8–10). Chapter 6 provides details of how the Sporting Capital Index scores are constructed.

Figure 3.2 shows how *in theory* external barriers interact with a person's sporting capital levels to moderate their probability of participating. It must

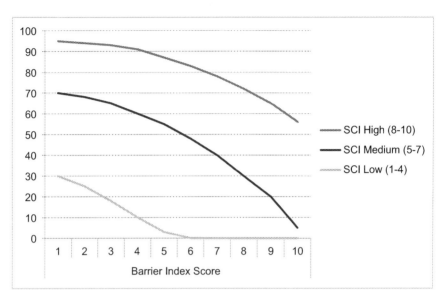

Figure 3.2 Theoretical perspective on the relationship between sporting capital, external barriers to participation in sport and probability of participating (%) (SCI is Sporting Capital Index score with 10 high and 1 low)

be emphasised that this is a theoretical construct and as yet lacks empirical validation. The theoretical proposition is that an individual with high levels of sporting capital will be more likely to overcome the same barriers faced by someone with low levels of sporting capital and hence for any given barrier level will have a higher probability of participating in sport. The consequences for public policy from this theoretical relationship are profound and have been touched on earlier in Chapter 2 when discussing the lack of impact of public policy investment in shifting overall population levels of participation in sport. For this reason they are worth elaborating further here before returning to this theme in the conclusions to this book. The implications of the proposed theoretical interaction between sporting capital, levels of constraints and barriers and probability of participating in sport are as follows:

• Barrier reduction will have a relatively very small impact on the probability of participating amongst those with the lowest level of sporting capital. Reducing barriers from 10 to 6 for this group will make no difference at all on their participation. Although a reduction in the barriers from 6 to 1 will increase their probability of participating, it will be a relatively small increase providing little marginal gain in the probability of participating. The maximum probability of participating for this group is 30 percent where barriers have been reduced to the lowest (and unrealistic) level. Put another way, 70 percent of those on the lowest levels of sporting capital will not participate in sport no matter how many resources are thrown at reducing barriers for them. The only way to substantially increase participation amongst the lowest sporting capital group is by increasing their level of sporting capital. For this group relatively small increases in sporting capital will make a very big difference to their probability of participating.

- The hypothesised relationship between barriers and the probability of participating for those on medium levels of sporting capital is very different to the one we see for those on low levels. The probability of participating is considerably higher at all barrier levels. At the lowest level the probability touches 70 percent but as barriers increase the probability decreases and at an increasing rate as barriers reach the mid range level of 5 and 6. The shape of this curve would theoretically point towards barrier reduction having a greater success for this middle range sporting capital group than it would for those on low levels of sporting capital. For this group the greatest return will be achieved by driving down barriers at the highest level, i.e. from 10 to 6 rather than from 5 to 1. However, even then barrier reduction alone will be limited in what it can achieve. The potential gains to be achieved from increasing sporting capital levels in this group still look relatively attractive with the possibility of substantial participation gains at all barrier levels.

- Those with the highest sporting capital scores have a relatively high probability of participating for all barrier levels. As barriers increase from the lowest levels there is a hypothesised slow decrease in the probability of participating. From a barrier level of 5 onwards there is a steeper decline in participation but less than we see for the middle range sporting capital group. This highest sporting capital group has the lowest potential gains to participation from increasing levels of sporting capital. For this group barrier reduction will make the biggest difference to participation, particularly at the upper end where a small decrease in barriers can have a relatively large impact on the probability of participating.

The 'Sports Participation Matrix' (SPM) shown in Figure 3.3 extends this thinking to explore a theorised relational dynamic model of sporting capital and external barriers to participation. The SPM embeds two key dynamics: 1) probability, on a scale from highly probable to highly improbable; and 2) stability on a scale from highly stable to highly unstable or fragile. As sporting capital increases, motivation to participate gets higher with associated increases in resilience to external barriers. As external barriers increase and sporting capital remains constant, then the probability of drop out increases. A person's location in the SPM shows a snapshot in time when the reality is of a temporal relationship constantly in flux. People's life circumstances change, particularly in times of transition, for example when leaving school; starting a new job; a new addition to the family; a time of illness and poor health; retirement from work; caring for an elderly relative (see Chapter 5). These changes in life circumstances can last for short or longer periods of time and can either work to increase barriers or more positively to decrease them. Levels of sporting capital also change, but tend to be more stable than life circumstances and less prone to catastrophic events. This is a positive insofar as once established sporting capital tends to persist but it also has a negative side; if not established early in life it is more difficult to shift later, requiring an investment of time and commitment to do so. However, the rewards of this investment of time and commitment, both to the individual and to society as a whole, of growing sporting capital are significant in terms of the increased probability of participation, the increased resilience to changes in external barriers and the

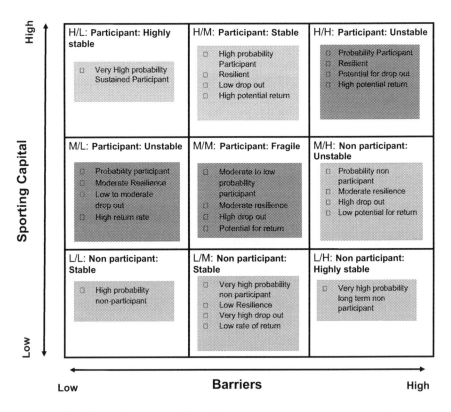

Figure 3.3 The 'Sports Participation Matrix'

likely return to sport once the external life circumstances return or move to conditions that are more favourable.

If we examine the SPM in more detail, some interesting observations and insights emerge. The top left-hand corner of the matrix and the bottom right-hand corner are polar opposites. Both are highly stable, one in the positive sense and one in the negative. In an ideal world public policy would want to move everyone out of the L/H box and into the H/L box, but clearly the distance between them is great. A characteristic of the matrix is that individual movement around it is most likely to be to an adjacent square, only in extreme circumstances is an individual likely to 'jump across' squares. Movement can either take a person in a positive or a negative direction. The nature of its 'nearest neighbour squares' impacts on the stability or fragility of a person's position in that square. The middle square is the most fragile as it has four nearest neighbour squares and movement can be in any of these directions. The bottom row of 'low sporting capital squares' are all associated with a high probability of being a non participant, and because sporting capital levels are not volatile is characterised by a level of stability. The only route to higher participant rates for individuals in the bottom left-hand square is to move their sporting capital up a level; even for individuals in the other two squares in the lowest row where barriers are moderate or high, barrier reduction is unlikely to pay much of a dividend as the low levels of sporting capital limit motivation to participate.

Participation in sport by those on medium levels of sporting capital (the middle row) is generally characterised as being unstable or fragile and is most impacted by the short term volatility of changes in the levels of barriers. Where barriers are low, an increase in sporting capital will lift an individual into the top left-hand sustained participant category; however, there is also a risk of moving sideways into the 'fragile' middle category or even worse to move downwards to the bottom left corner square should levels of sporting capital decrease.

The top right- hand square is an interesting one. An individual in this square is resilient to barriers because of their high level of sporting capital, so in the face of barriers that would put most people off participating in sport they will persist. However, if the barriers remain high and are sustained over a moderate period of time, the probability is that the individual will start to participate less as the barriers start to chip away at their enjoyment and motivation. Their sporting capital levels are, however, durable and should the barriers reduce due for example to a change in life circumstances, they will quickly bounce back to becoming a regular participant – i.e. move into the 'H/M: Participant Stable square'. However, there is a possibility with high barriers persisting over a long period of time that sporting capital will slowly decline until a tipping point is reached and the individual will drop into the square below with the much higher probability of becoming a non participant.

From a macro policy perspective the ideal is to move the population into the top row boxes 'H/L and H/M' of sustained and stable participation with individuals who have high levels of sporting capital and low to moderate barriers. The reality is that most of the population are some distance (at least two moves) away from this. A pragmatic approach to public policy would suggest the best returns would be to focus on the 'H/H; M/L and MM boxes' where any positive shift particularly in sporting capital but also in barrier reduction could pay large dividends. This is not to justify consigning those in the bottom row boxes, 'L/L; L/M; L/H' and right hand middle row box 'M/H' to public policy neglect. These individuals invariably face the greatest challenges associated with poverty, poor health, social isolation and neighbourhood deprivation. Here intervention should focus predominantly on encouraging physically active lifestyle changes as a route to improved health and social engagement and in the longer term perhaps as a movement up the matrix and back into sport.

The SPM demonstrates that effective public policy intervention in community sport is achieved through an approach that balances investment in building sporting capital with investment in external barrier reduction. However, there are two crucial points which flow from the theory of sporting capital that I would argue are not being adequately addressed by public policy in community sport as it has been framed over the last 40 years or so. The first, stated above and demonstrated in the SPM, is that a large number of people in the population, the evidence from my empirical work documented in Chapter 6 suggests that it is in the order of 25 percent to 30 percent of the adult population, have levels of sporting capital that are so low that they will have a very limited response to any reduction in barriers to participation. The second point and one which I presented theoretically in Figure 3.2 is that the maximum return on population level participation in sport is ultimately severely constrained by a predominant focus on external barrier reduction. *Only societal wide shifts in levels of sporting capital can create the potential to achieve substantive changes in population levels of sustained participation in sport.*

Sporting capital is a 'universal theory' at least insofar as it is internationally transferable and applicable across 'economically developed countries'. To this extent it lends itself to comparative international research. From a theoretical perspective it is anticipated that those countries with the highest levels of participation will also have the highest levels of sporting capital. Empirical research is required to test this proposition and to explore to what degree sporting capital and participation rates are related in different countries and across different socio-demographic groups. In those countries that have relatively high levels of sporting capital it would be of significant policy interest to explore the reasons for this which, for example, might include advantages in early learning experiences; family influences; school environments and teaching; the availability and quality of sports clubs and coaching; community outreach; the quality and accessibility of sporting environments; and the nature of the sport experience (see Chapter 8). But the relationship between sporting capital and participation rates may not always be that simple. If for example, and contrary to expectation, comparative research showed that sporting capital levels in those countries with the highest levels of participation are equivalent to or lower than those found in countries with relatively low rates of participation (or for any given level of sporting capital participation rates are higher), then it will point to the likelihood that external barriers/constraints to participation are lower in these countries – e.g. there is better facility supply, relatively lower prices, better childcare, more workplace opportunities and again this would lead to a fruitful line of enquiry.

Figure 3.4 pulls all the elements referred to in this chapter together to form a coherent sporting capital theory of change. Read from left to right a socialisation process (interpreted as the wider socio-cultural context) impacts on and shapes the three sporting capital domains: physiological, psychological and social, which in turn interact to create an individual's stock of sporting capital. The stock of sporting capital impacts on and creates a level of motivation to take part in sport. The translation of motivation into actual behaviour is mediated or filtered through external barriers; if the motivation is sufficiently high or the barriers sufficiently low, then an individual will participate in sport. If the barriers relative to motivation are sufficient to prevent participation, there is the potential for a reinforcement of the negative aspects of psychological affect, weakening of sporting social connections and reductions in physical competence and health status. Where external barriers are overcome, there is the potential for either

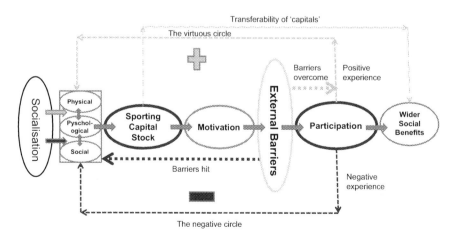

Figure 3.4 Sporting capital theory of change

a positive or negative feedback loop dependent upon the quality of the participation experience. A positive experience can build sporting capital while a negative experience can reduce it. Finally as part of a virtuous circle, positive participation experiences build sporting capital which through the potential for transferability of capitals can, given the right conditions, impact positively on wider societal benefits such as public health, human, social and cultural capital.

To conclude this chapter it is worth summarising those aspects of sporting capital theory that I believe can make a real difference to public policy and practice in sports development. The following provides a synopsis of the theoretical characteristics of sporting capital that have important implications for public policy and practice:

- Sporting capital is a universal theory that provides a holistic and integrated view of the determinants of participation that span the psychological, social and physiological characteristics of a persons' identity, lifestyle and relationship to others.
- The theory provides a common ground and a common language for all sports development, establishing the 'big picture' that sets the guiding principles and agendas for joined up action, whether in schools, colleges, local outreach, local authorities, national governing bodies of sport, national sport development agencies or government departments.
- Although sporting capital can appreciate and depreciate, it is by its nature more durable than participation which is characterised by high levels of flux. As a consequence it shifts the focus of public policy from the short-term objective of increasing an individual's current participation in sport to one of building the capacity to participate in sport now and over the longer term. In this sense it is a theory that values capacity building and individual empowerment.
- It is anticipated that increased sporting capital leads to more frequent and diverse participation in sport and, in turn, more frequent and sustained participation impacts positively to build and reinforce sporting capital in a virtuous feedback loop.
- It is expected that high quality sporting experiences are likely to have a more positive impact on sporting capital than mediocre ones, while poor quality experiences can have a negative impact leading to depreciation in the levels of sporting capital and over time to drop out and sedentary behaviours.
- Evidence suggests (see Chapter 5) that significant aspects of sporting capital such as physical competency and self efficacy are developed at a very young age, involve a socialisation process with boys much more likely to build sporting capital than girls and the more socio-economically advantaged having higher levels than those from lower socio-economic groups and can depreciate, or less likely build, over time and with age.

- It creates the potential to better understand the key influences that shape an individual's relationship to sport, when and how they occur and in what context. In particular it emphasises the early formative years in a young persons' life when sporting capital is most likely to be built and the factors that lead to its growth and, for many, what causes depreciation in sporting capital and associated drop out through the life-course.
- Although it stresses the importance of the early formative years, the theory holds out the potential for later life interventions that seek to build or rebuild sporting capital to levels that instigate and sustain participation in sport for many who have previously been neglected in public policy (see Chapter 5).
- The theory provides a better understanding of how external barriers and constraints that impact on participation and personal factors combine to determine an individual's level of sporting capital and how they interact to determine the likelihood of participating in sport. It suggests that public policy intervention must strike the right balance between barrier reduction and sporting capital increase if it is to optimise participation rates. The theory suggests that relatively modest increases in sporting capital levels across the population could make significant shifts in overall participation rates in sport.
- It provides the potential to customise (match) interventions to the sporting capital profile of an individual (or perhaps more realistically groups of individuals), to build those aspects of capital that are weak, to avoid offering sport in ways that could be counter-productive – turning people off rather than on to sport – and to focus on barrier reduction only where appropriate and likely to be effective.

References

Bakera, J. and Horton, S., 2004. A review of primary and secondary influences on sport expertise. *High Ability Studies*, 15(2), pp. 211–228. http://dx.doi.org/10.1080/1359813042000314781

BBC, 2010. *Cameron and Clegg set out 'big society' policy ideas*. Available at: <http://news.bbc.co.uk/1/hi/uk_politics/8688860.stm> [accessed 9th January 2017].

Becker, G., 1964. *Human capital: A theoretical and empirical analysis, with special reference to education*. New York: National Bureau of Economic Research; Distributed by Columbia University Press.

Bourdieu, P., 1986. The forms of capital. In: J. Richardson, ed. *Handbook of theory and research for the sociology of education*. New York: Greenwood, pp. 241–258.

The Cabinet Office, 2010. *Building the big society*. Available at: <www.cabinetoffice.gov.uk/content/big-society-overview>.

Coalter, F., 2007. *A wider social role for sport: Who's keeping the score*. London: Routledge.

Crawford, D. W. and Godbey, G., 1987. Reconceptualizing barriers to family leisure. *Leisure Sciences*, 9(2), pp. 119–127.

Crawford, D. W., Jackson, E. L. and Godbey, G., 1991. A hierarchical model of leisure constraints. *Leisure Sciences*, 13(4), pp. 309–320.

Csikszentmihalyi, M., 1978. Attention and the holistic approach to behaviour. In: K. S. Pope and J. L. Singer, eds. *The stream of consciousness: Scientific investigations into the flow of human experience.* New York: Plenum Publishing, pp. 335–385.

Csikszentmihalyi, M., 1990. *Flow: The psychology of optimal experience.* New York: Harper & Row.

Csikszentmihalyi, M. and Nakamura, J., 1989. The dynamics of intrinsic motivation: A study of adolescents. In: C. Ames and R. Ames, eds. *Research on motivation in education, vol. 3: Goals and cognitions.* New York: Academic Press, pp. 45–71.

De Graaf, N. D., De Graaf, P. M. and Kraaykamp, G., 2000. Parental cultural capital and educational attainment in the Netherlands: A refinement of the cultural capital perspective. *Sociology of Education*, 73(2), pp. 92–111.

Driscoll, K. and Wood, L., 1999. *Sporting capital: Changes and challenges for rural communities in Victoria.* Melbourne: Centre for Applied Social Research, RMIT.

Duckworth, A. L., Peterson, C., Matthews, M. D. and Kelly, D. R., 2007. Grit: Perseverance and passion for long – term goals. *Journal of Personality and Social Psychology*, 92(6), pp. 1087–1101.

Eurostat, 2014. *Sport and physical activity report.* Special Eurobarometer 412. Brussels: European Commission.

Fisher, K., 2002. *Chewing the fat: The story time diaries tell about physical activity in the United Kingdom.* Working Papers of the Institute for Social and Economic Research, Paper 2002–13. Colchester: University of Essex.

Gershuny, J., 2003. *Time, through the lifecourse, in the family.* ISER Working Paper 2003–3; Colchester: University of Essex.

Goldthorpe, J. H., undated. *Cultural capital: Some critical observations.* Sociology Working Papers Paper Number 2007–07. Oxford: Department of Sociology University of Oxford. Available at: <www.sociology.ox.ac.uk/materials/papers/swp07_07.pdf> [accessed 4th January 2017].

Halsey, A. H., Heath, A. F. and Ridge, J. M., 1980. *Origins and destinations.* Oxford: Clarendon Press.

Haworth, J., 1993. Skills-challenge relationships and psychological well-being in everyday life. *Society & Leisure*, 16(1), pp. 115–128.

Jackson, E. L., Crawford, D. W. and Godbey, G., 1993. Negotiation of leisure constraints. *Leisure Sciences*, 15(1), pp. 1–11.

Jackson, S. A., Kimiecik, J. C., Ford, S. and Marsh, H. W., 1998. Psychological correlates of flow in sport. *Journal of Sport & Exercise Psychology*, 20(4), pp. 358–378.

Matthews, P., Xu, D., Matusiak, M. and Prior, G., 2016. *Taking part: Findings from the longitudinal survey waves 1 to 3.* April. TNS BMRB. London: Department for Culture Media and Sport.

Nakamura, J. and Csikszentmihalyi, M., 2005. The concept of flow. In: C. R. Snyder and S. J. Lopez, eds. *Handbook of positive psychology.* New York: Oxford University Press, pp. 89–105.

Nicholson, M. and Hoye, R. eds., 2008. *Sport and social capital.* Oxford: Butterworth-Heinemann.

Putnam, R. D., 2000. *Bowling alone: The collapse and revival of American community*. New York: Simon and Schuster.

Rowe, N. F., 2015. Sporting capital: A theoretical and empirical analysis of sport participation determinants and its application to sports development policy and practice. *International Journal of Sport Policy and Politics*, 7(1), pp. 43–61.

Shilling, C., 1991. Educating the body: Physical capital and the production of social inequalities. *Sociology*, 25(4), pp. 653–672.

Shilling, C., 1993. *The body and social theory*. London: Sage.

Stempel, C., 2006. Gender, social class, and the sporting capital–economic capital nexus. *Sociology of Sport Journal*, 23(3), pp. 273–292.

Stuij, M., 2015. Habitus and social class: A case study on socialisation into sports and exercise. *Sport, Education and Society*, 20(6), pp. 780–798. http://dx.doi.org/10.1080/13573322.2013.827568

Tlili, A. and Obsiye, M., 2014. What is Coleman's social capital the name of? A critique of a not very social capital. *Critical Sociology*, 40(4), pp. 551–574.

Warde, A., 2006. Cultural capital and the place for sport. *Cultural Trends*, 15(2–3), pp. 107–122.

Chapter 4

Theories of sport development and behaviour change – why do we need yet another theory?

I have made it clear from the outset that although the theory of sporting capital is new in its holistic conceptualisation of sport-related behaviour and in its parallels to other forms of 'capital', its constituent parts are familiar and well-rehearsed with a large body of evidence. This is only to be expected and in no way undermines or devalues the power of the theory to shed new light on sporting behaviours, their determinants and by implication our ability to intervene to influence and shape them. In fact it strengthens it. I have also suggested that sporting capital theory does not sit in isolation disconnected from theories of behaviour change particularly as they relate to physical activity and other lifestyle behaviours. What I have stressed is the specificity of sporting capital theory to the socio-cultural phenomenon that is community sport and I argue in this chapter that the shoehorning of these other theories to apply directly to sport has significant limitations.

In the pages that follow I review a number of prominent theories and how they relate to sporting capital. In so doing I have not attempted to provide a comprehensive account or in-depth critique, which could be a book in its own right. My ambition here, more limited but no less important in the context of this book, is to show that the theory of sporting capital rather than contradicting or seeking to devalue other theories in most cases incorporates, builds on or adapts them to provide a specificity and relevance to sporting behaviour change and to public policy intervention that was previously absent. I conclude the chapter by placing the locus of the theory of sporting capital in the wider context of a philosophical approach to human development which sees the individual as realising their potential to 'thrive' through enhanced capacities which unlock choice and provide a sense of agency, i.e. an empowering sense of control and impact on their life and the circumstances surrounding it.

Theories of sport development

Perhaps the earliest attempt to create a theoretical basis for sports development policy and practice was the 'Sports Development Continuum' made up of a pyramid moving from the bottom upwards of: 'Foundation', involving young people to include play activities and basic movement skills; 'Participation', playing sport for fun, enjoyment, health and fitness; 'Performance', playing at club, county, regional level in a given sport; and 'Excellence', playing at a national and international standard. This 'model' of sports development featured extensively in the policy narrative during the late 1980s and 1990s (Houlihan, 2000). Although prevalent in public policy it has not, however, been without its critics. Kirk and Gorely (2000, p. 123) highlighted the limitations of the 'standard model' when applied to the links between physical education, sport performance and active lifestyles,

> There is no guarantee that geometry models real life. If children are taught poorly at the base, all we have is a large number of poor performers. Even if they are taught well, the pyramid does not seem to be a good way of thinking about the young performers' progress.

In a similar vein Bailey (2007, p. 370) questioned the role of school physical education as a preparation for elite performance in sport, i.e. movement up the sports development continuum to its pinnacle, by raising "the 'empirical difficulty' associated with the fact that only 0.001 percent of the current school population could possibility reach the highest level." Taking a narrower talent development perspective, Bailey et al. (2010, p. 15) observe that,

> Pyramid models presume that selection for progressively higher levels within the system are based on merit, while in practice, participation is mediated by a host of psychosocial and environmental factors, such as the ability to take part in the first place.

A revised and perhaps more socio-ecologically sound version of the model that better reflected the less hierarchical nature of the relationship between participation and performance was presented as early as 1991 by the then Sports Council (see Houlihan and White, 2002, p. 41). As recently as 2007 a 'Church Model' has been proposed by Scheerder et al. (2011); however, these variants on the development continuum 'triangle' have had less traction than the attractive simplicity of the original and remain, like the original, fundamentally descriptive rather than explanatory in nature.

At the time of its introduction the sports development continuum model provided a helpful way for public policy to conceptualise engagement in sport as an interconnected system. However, it was a product of its time which oversimplified the diversity of involvement and motivations for engagement in sport; led to some misconceptions about scale and the idea of progression through hierarchies of engagement; failed to represent in any meaningful way the context and mediators of engagement in sport; and as a descriptive model did not fully represent or explain the dynamic process of how individuals move up, down and around the pyramid and the factors that influence these movements (see for example the critique by Scheerder et al., 2011). Most pertinent to this review, the 'pyramid model' says little if anything about the differentiating factors that lead to drop out or sustained lifelong participation in sport.

Other sport development models have been orientated more towards athlete development and talent pathways than to the social processes relevant to individual behaviour in the wider community. Perhaps the most notable and influential of these models of 'participant development' is the Long Term Athlete Development Model (LTAD) associated with the ideas and theories of Istvan Balyi (Balyi and Hamilton, 2000). Balyi's model of LTAD references age-specific phases of athlete development through which individuals progress en route to achieving elite performance. 'Athletes' progress from the first 'FUNdamentals' phase for young people aged 5 to 9 years where the main objective should be the overall development of physical capacities and fundamental movement skills through to a fifth phase of 'Training to win' where the main objective should be to maximise fitness preparation and sport/event-specific skills, as well as performance. The final sixth phase is one Balyi refers to as 'Retirement and Retainment' where the main objective should be to retain athletes for coaching, officiating, sport administration and so on. Whereas LTAD is a very physiologically oriented model, Côté's 'Developmental Model of Sport Participation' (DMSP) (Côté, 1999; Côté and Fraser-Thomas, 2007) is predominantly a psychological one. Côté's model refers to three stages of athlete development as follows:

- The sampling phase (6–12 years): when children are given the opportunity to sample a range of sports, develop a foundation of fundamental movement skills and experience sport as a source of fun and excitement. In the sampling years parents are responsible for getting their children interested in sport and the selection of a particular sport is less important than the amount of fun it provides.
- The specialising phase (13–15 years): when the child begins to focus on a smaller number of sports and, while fun and enjoyment are still vital, sport-specific skill development emerges as an important characteristic of sport engagement. The quality of the experience and positive feedback is important in encouraging young teenagers to stay involved and to specialise in a particular sport.
- The investment phase (16+ years): When the child becomes committed to achieving a high level of performance in a specific sport and the strategic, competitive and skill development elements of sport emerges as the most important. The number of hours of intense training increases drastically, while the number of hours of informal 'play' type activity decreases.

Côté's model extends to the possibility of recreational involvement or potential drop out in the 'specialising phase' and in this sense is a more general model of sporting engagement and behaviours than LTAD although still having its roots in athlete development pathways and progression.

Bailey and Morley's (2006) model of Talent Development takes a more multi-dimensional perspective on the factors that underpin sporting success. They distinguish between the expression of abilities and the progressive emergence of these abilities into certain formalised outcomes. Abilities are developed within certain domains that are refined, combined and elaborated into particular behaviours, such as sporting success. These abilities are: psychomotor ability (revealed through movement and the physical performance of skills); interpersonal ability (exhibited in social contexts and is the basis of leadership, teamwork and similar concepts); intrapersonal ability (underpins an individual's capacity for self-control, self efficacy and emotional intelligence); cognitive ability (shown in tactical settings, as well as knowledge and understanding of central physical educational concepts); creative ability (evidenced when learners respond to challenges and tasks with fluency, originality and sensitivity to problems).

Theories of physical activity behaviour change

The models referred to above have their antecedents in 'athlete development' and 'talent pathways'. They take relatively narrow perspectives on individual behaviour orientated more towards performance outcomes and sporting success than broader behaviour change, although they touch on aspects of the sport experience such as 'fun', 'sampling', and 'basic skills and abilities' that do read across and have relevance to the theory of sporting capital. Over recent years, however, sports development policy and practice has increasingly turned its attention to theories related to physical activity behaviour change. This is in part a response to the narrow focus of the 'sport theories' and in part because of the too broad a focus of the 'sports development continuum' as a practical theory to explain individual behavioural choices. However, it is more broadly to be explained by the increasing realisation that the ambition of public policy in community sport to increase, widen and sustain participation is essentially an outcome focused on effecting mass behaviour change that is similar in kind to the wider public policy focus on preventative health behaviours. The nearest neighbour to sport in public policy terms is the promotion of physical activity with sport itself being a constituent part of the physical activity agenda and an important contributor to health outcomes in its own right (see Chapter 2). It is not surprising, therefore, that sport policy and development has over recent years looked towards theories of behaviour change, particularly as they relate to physical activity behaviours (Foster et al., 2005).

A number of theories of behaviour change have been used to guide the design and implementation of physical activity interventions. Four theories have been particularly prominent: the 'theory of reasoned action'; the 'theory of planned behaviour'; 'social cognitive theory'; and the 'transtheoretical/stages of change model', and these are discussed below.

The theory of reasoned action (TRA) (Fishbein and Azjen, 1975) assumes that individuals consider the consequences of behaviour before performing the particular behaviour. A person's intention is determined both by their own attitudes towards the behaviour together with the influence of societal norms and expectations about the behaviour. As a result, intention is an important factor in determining behaviour and behavioural change. The theory of reasoned action suggests that the probability of engaging in physical activity would be increased if: a person predicts that physical activity will be enjoyable; physical activity will lead to only valued positive outcomes and minimal discomfort or harm; a person's social network will want them to be physically active; and a persons' social network is physically active.

Ajzen (1985) expanded upon the theory of reasoned action, formulating the theory of planned behaviour (TPB), which also emphasises the role of intention in behaviour but adds the dimensions of perceived control over the factors affecting the behaviour and the levels of self efficacy to overcome the barriers preventing the behaviour or making it more difficult. The TPB includes the proposition that a greater degree a person perceives they have control over a behaviour, the more effort they will put into performing it. So if a person perceived that becoming more active would be reasonably easy, they were confident they could do it and they perceived there were plenty of opportunities to do it, they would have a high intention to be active. A meta analysis of studies of the TRA and TPB carried out by Hausenblas and colleagues at the University of Western Ontario (Hausenblas, Carron and Mack, 1997) concluded that, "The constructs embedded in the TPB – attitude, subjective norm, perceived behavioral control, and intention – have considerable utility in predicting and explaining exercise behaviour" (p. 46). They also go on to say that, "The results from the present study provide strong evidence that the theory of reasoned action is a good theory; its extension, the theory of planned behaviour, is an even better theory" (p. 46).

According to the social cognitive theory developed by Bandura (1986), behaviour change is determined by environmental, personal and behavioural elements with each factor interacting to affect each of the others. An individual's environment affects the development of personal characteristics as well as the person's behaviour, and an individual's behaviour may change their environment as well as the way the individual thinks or feels. Two kinds of outcomes are central to social cognitive theory: outcome expectations and efficacy expectations. The outcome expectations are framed in terms of beliefs about whether a given behaviour is likely to lead to certain outcomes both in relation to anticipated personal gains and losses and in terms of social responses or approval or disapproval. Positive outcomes serve as incentives and negative ones as disincentives. As Bandura (1998, p. 628) says:

> People do not behave like weathervanes, constantly shifting to whatever social influences happen to impinge on them at the moment. They adopt personal standards and regulate their behavior by their self-sanctions. They do things that give them self-satisfaction and self-worth, and refrain from behaving in ways that breed self dissatisfaction. . . . Evaluative self-sanction is one of the more influential regulators of human behavior but typically neglected in models of personal change.

Self efficacy expectations refer to a person's perception of how capable they are of performing a behaviour that will lead to desirable outcomes. Self efficacy expectations are influenced by: previous experience and mastery over those experiences; vicarious experience of observing the behaviour performed by others similar to the observer; verbal persuasion in the form of encouragement; and physiological arousal which in the context of physical activity refers to the extent an individual interprets sweating and increased heart rate as negative signs of vulnerability (Bandura, 1998). According to Bandura (2001, p. 10), "Efficacy beliefs are the foundation of human agency. Unless people believe they can produce desired results and forestall detrimental ones by their actions, they have little incentive to act or to persevere in the face of difficulties."

The theme of the transtheoretical/stages of change model (Prochaska, Diclemente and Norcross, 1992; Prochaska and Velicer, 1997) is that behaviour change involves movement through a series of stages before sustained change is achieved. The entry point is the 'pre-contemplation' stage, where an individual may or may not be aware of a problem but has no thought of changing their behaviour. From 'pre-contemplation' to 'contemplation', the individual develops a desire to change a behaviour. During 'preparation', the individual intends to change the behaviour within the near future, and during the 'action' stage, the individual begins to exhibit new behaviour consistently. An individual finally enters the 'maintenance' stage once they exhibit the new behaviour consistently for over six months. Relapse is the rule rather than the exception in behaviour change and most people will move around the different stages a number of times before achieving lasting change. The model emphasises the importance of matching the intervention style and strategy to the individual's stage of change, although as Foster et al. (2005, p. 22) note, "although the model is intuitively appealing and has received much support from practitioners, the research evidence supporting a stage-based approach (to interventions) over a non-stage-based one is equivocal." Bandura (1998, p. 631) provides a highly critical assessment of 'stages of change theories' in positing that,

> The stage view substitutes a categorical approach for a process model of human adaptation and change. Contrary to claims, shift from one descriptive category of intention to another, or from a short duration of behavior to a longer duration does not make the stage approach a 'dynamic process model'. Even a genuine stage theory is at best a descriptive device rather than an explanatory one.

The transtheoretical model is very much a 'clinical model' insofar as its origins and much of the research underpinning it have been drawn from a medical health promotion context, particularly as it relates to smoking cessation, dietary change and physical activity/exercise promotion. A search for evidence of the application of the transtheoretical model to changes in 'sport' behaviour within a paradigm that sits outside of a medical model shows a dearth of evidence in this aspect of behaviour change.

Foster et al. (2005) in reviewing the various models of behaviour change go on to discuss the merits of a more holistic 'trans-disciplinary' model of physical activity as proposed by King et al. (2002) that encompasses personal, social and environmental constructs. This model integrates the relationship between an individual's biological dispositions (genetic make-up) their attitudes, beliefs, knowledge and skills and how these interact with the physical and social environment as well as previous and current physical activity behaviour. Relationships are 'bi-directional' so, for example, increased physical activity increases endurance capacity, strength and functional capacity making a wider range of physical activities less demanding and thereby more attractive. In the social and community context greater prevalence in a neighbourhood of cycling and walking, for example, can lead to less car dependency which leads to greater safety and in turn increases cycling and walking – a virtuous feedback loop.

Foster et al. (2005) go on to stress the importance the built environment plays in affecting physical activity behaviour change, and following King et al. (2002), propose the need for a trans-disciplinary approach that goes beyond personal level factors to include environmental and cultural ones. In the concluding sections of their report (Foster et al., p. 43), Hillsdon proposes an integrated model where desired participation outcomes are determined by a complex interaction of 'neighbourhood' variables such as residential density, safety and the availability of parks, leisure centres and other places for physical activity with individual demographic, social community network and psychological variables. This trans-disciplinary perspective can trace its antecedents to the biopsychosocial model that was initially developed in the context of disease progression and outcomes (Engel, 1977). The biopsychosocial model takes a broad integrated philosophical view about human development and counters the uni-dimensional biological model that had previously dominated medicine. The model is as much if not more about intervention and clinical care as it is about disease causation. Bailey et al. (2010) in a review commissioned by SportsCoach UK take this perspective and extend its application to a 'sport participant model' that refers to the biological, psychological and social domains and their interaction. The emphasis throughout is the link to performance and 'coaching frameworks', but this direction of thinking is consistent with and lends much to the theory of sporting capital. Interestingly Bailey et al. (2010, p. 89) conclude that

> the current state of research in this crucial area does not provide a sufficiently comprehensive understanding of the key interactions between domains, nor provide a sufficiently firm base for future progress and application. Against this backdrop, we suggest our review of the scientific literature can act as a starting point for further exploration.

This brief review of theoretical models that have been prevalent in sport and physical activity behaviour change provides an important reference point for the development of the theoretical propositions underpinning 'sporting capital'. Although each of the theories discussed above make a contribution to how we frame our thinking and approach to public policy in sport and recreation, it becomes quickly apparent that the application of the theories to the public policy domain of community sport development is not a perfect fit. The 'sport theories' are orientated towards elite sport success and associated talent identification, development and pathways and say little about the determinants and influences that lead to inactivity, drop out from sport at an early age or a failure to sustain sporting activity through the life-course. The theories borrowed from the wider health and physical activity public policy domains have their strength in being grounded in the more fundamental drivers and determinants of behaviour change but lack the cultural and institutional specificity that distinguishes sport from informal exercise and activity in everyday life. Sport is itself a socio-cultural construct and any effective theory of sporting behaviour and its determinants must embed these aspects of the very nature of sport as an integral part of the theory. Sporting capital does just this by addressing the particular and sport-specific factors that are influential in both the decision to participate in sport at any given time but also most importantly the likelihood of sustaining that participation over time.

Sporting capital: a synthesis of sport and physical activity theories

The locus for sporting capital theory is not confined to or dominated by any one theoretical construct reviewed in this chapter. Its strength lies in the way that it spans elements of both the 'sport' theories' and the 'physical activity behaviour change' theories to provide a synthesis of the two. Key elements of the theories reviewed are prominent in the theory of sporting capital; for example the importance of self efficacy, identity and self confidence, which are key ingredients in the psychological domain; the importance of relationships, social support networks, interaction with family, peers, teachers, coaches and role models constituted in the social domain; and the importance of physical skills and mastery, physical literacy and general health status all constituent parts of the physiological domain. Its scope provides for a socio-ecological perspective extending from the intrapersonal to the interpersonal to the community and wider cultural context. It is transdisciplinary, including and integrating psychology, sociology, behavioural and market economics, culture and anthropology and political science and biology. Sporting capital theory embraces aspects of motivational theory in terms of attitudes, beliefs, knowledge and skills, intention, outcome expectations, self evaluation, reinforcement, quality of experience, agency and mediating and moderating factors. It is contextualised and related to wider cultural, institutional and environmental variables whether defined as external barriers and constraints or as opportunities.

To interpret sporting capital theory as purely an individual behavioural theory would be to misunderstand its central constructs and propositions. Yes, the theory focuses on the capacities of individuals as they relate to sport in terms of physical abilities and health, psychological characteristics of self confidence, self efficacy and identity and on social connections and support. However, it recognises that the shaping of these behaviours is a consequence of the intersection of a wide array of cultural, institutional and environmental factors that sit outside the direct control of any one individual 'actor'. In so doing it fully acknowledges that the 'solution' to the uneven distribution of sporting capital across the population and the low levels found in certain groups and individuals can only be found by a systematic approach to the problem that responds to individual agency contextualised by community and environmental and wider socio-cultural structures. As Kohl and colleagues (2012, p. 302) conclude in their Lancet article on the 'pandemic of global levels of physical inactivity',

> Complete understanding of all stakeholders, their interactions, and how their interactions make up the whole is crucial to understanding of the systems that impede progress on physical activity. Such a task again will necessitate coordination, communication, and partnership development across the myriad of stakeholders who can affect change.

'Community sport', albeit a sub-system of the wider domain of 'physical activity', is complex and multi-faceted in its own right. It has the characteristics of a 'wicked problem' (Rittel and Webber, 1973) described earlier in

Chapter 2. A systems approach to building sporting capital needs to match this complexity with complexity; to recognise that policy, environment (including physical, cultural and institutional) and individual characteristics all bear down to influence and shape a person's level of sporting capital. An effective response needs to reflect and engage in these interrelationships. It needs to balance barrier reduction with individual capacity building; to identify key agencies, roles, responsibilities and interactions and to understand that while many come from the world of 'sports development', many others inhabit tangential or touching worlds of health promotion, education, community development, social care, youth offending and youth services, environmental and town planning, rural development and corporate business interests.

Sporting capital theory is not a neutral theory insofar as it takes a normative position on the value of sport to society. It doesn't just describe what is but also references what could be and, to an extent, what should be. Sporting capital provides the individual with enhanced capacity to achieve higher order outcomes of self development and self actualisation (Maslow, 1954). Tay and Diener's (2011) empirical research across 123 countries supported the conclusion of earlier researchers (Sirgy and Wu, 2009, p. 363) that a 'balance in life' is associated with increases in subjective well-being (SWB) and quality of life,

> many resources, including hours of social time, show declining marginal utility just as money does. Thus, because people need to fulfill a variety of needs, it is likely that a mix of daily activities that includes mastery, social relationships, and the meeting of physical needs is required for optimal SWB.

It is interesting that sporting capital ticks all three of these boxes. In its broadest sense sporting capital theory takes a human development perspective defined in a report by the United Nations (1998, p. 14) as,

> a process of enlarging people's choices . . . achieved by expanding human capabilities and functionings . . . (it) goes further: (than basic requirements of a long and healthy life, knowledge and access to resources): essential areas of choice highly valued by people range from political, economic and social opportunities to being creative and productive to enjoying self respect, empowerment and sense of belonging to a community.

Linked to the broad concept of human development is that of 'thriving' which has been applied in particular to the developmental trajectories of adolescence when individuals undergo a period of "pronounced and often dramatic changes involving all the individual's biological, psychological, behavioural and social functioning" (King et al., 2005, p. 95). 'Thriving' provides a perspective on human development that goes beyond the deficit model to explore potential for growth, self actualisation and wider contribution to society. Benson and Scales (2009, p. 91) conceptualise the thriving process as

> animated by a passion for, and the exercise of action to nurture a self-identified interest, skill, or capacity. It could be anything from the love of writing poetry to disassembling and rebuilding car engines. We have begun to refer to this self-identified core passion (a central component of thriving) as a person's 'spark'. The pursuit and exercise of this interest is done for its own sake. The motivation is intrinsic, not extrinsic. Time engaged in pursuing this passionate interest often generates a kind of affect akin to joy.

In his forward to the revised edition of his seminal publication on 'The Joyless Economy', Scitovsky (1992, p. *viii*) takes a similar perspective referring to how "Advancing civilisation would advance our happiness if our education for enjoying leisure by putting it to good use increased in step with the increase in our leisure."

In concluding this chapter I do not want to come across as a 'sport evangelist' who castigates or belittles all those who do not share my interest or desire to take part in sport or to suggest that in some way this is a personal inadequacy or sign of individual failure. Everyone has the right to choose to take part or not to take part in sport, which after all is a discretionary leisure activity, in the same way that they might choose not to enjoy certain types of music, poetry or not to take up gardening or to visit museums. My view, however, is that the conscious decision to not take part should be made from a position of strength, i.e. from a position where the individual has the necessary skills, positive psychological affect and supportive social connections combined with appropriate opportunities and environments that make sport possible, rewarding and life enhancing. That is, to make the decision from a position of relatively high levels of sporting capital. I also believe, although accept that it has yet to be proven, that achieving at least moderate levels of sporting capital is well within the reach of each and every one of us. I have no doubt that sustained participation in sport, and particularly sport in a social and community context, helps a person to thrive by contributing to a well-rounded life in which a person can realise their potential, build their capabilities and express themselves physically. I also believe the obverse of this argument applies, that we should not live in a society where for many people the pleasure and self expression that can be derived from participation in sport is denied them because of what is for them a rational response to a lack of ability, poor self confidence and lack of social support combined with what appear to be insurmountable constraints and negative external environments.

In a society that values and invests in sporting capital the likelihood of lifelong participation in sport is enhanced, the chances of people returning to sport after a break are increased and the benefits to wider society are promoted. To put it succinctly, building levels of sporting capital amongst young people should be viewed as a right just as building human capital by access to education is a right. Sustaining and topping up sporting capital into adulthood and older age if not a right is certainly a sound public investment in a society that values individual and societal well-being and the opportunity for its citizens to live full and meaningful lives. 'Sporting capital for all' is a goal that as a society we should endorse and mobilise our efforts to achieve.

References

Ajzen, I., 1985. From intentions to actions: A theory of planned behavior. In: J. Kuhl and J. Beckman, eds. *Action-control: From cognition to behavior*. New York: Springer, pp. 11–39.

Bailey, R., 2007. Talent development and the luck problem. *Sport, Ethics and Philosophy*, 1(3), pp. 367–377. http://dx.doi.org/10.1080/17511320701676999

Bailey, R., Collins, D., Ford, P., MacNamara, A., Toms, M. and Pearce, G., 2010. *Participant development in sport: An academic review*. Leeds: Sports Coach UK.

Bailey, R. and Morley, D., 2006. Towards a model of talent development in physical education. *Sport, Education and Society*, 11(3), pp. 211–230. http://dx.doi.org/10.1080/13573320600813366

Balyi, I. and Hamilton, A., 2000. A key to success: Long-term athlete development. *Sport Coach* (Canberra, Australia), 23(1), pp. 10–32.

Bandura, A., 1986. *Social foundations of thought and action, a social cognitive theory*. Englewood Cliffs, NJ: Prentice Hall.

Bandura, A., 1998. Health promotion from the perspective of social cognitive theory. *Psychology and Health*, 13(4), pp. 623–649.

Bandura, A., 2001. Social cognitive theory: An agentic perspective. *Annual Review of Psychology*, 52, pp. 1–26.

Benson, P. and Scales, P., 2009. The definition and preliminary measurement of thriving in adolescence. *The Journal of Positive Psychology*, 4(1), pp. 85–104.

Côté, J., 1999. The influence of the family in the development of talent in sport. *Sport Psychologist*, 13(4), pp. 395–417.

Côté, J. and Fraser-Thomas, J., 2007. Youth involvement in sport. In: P. Crocker, ed. *Introduction to sport psychology: A Canadian perspective*. Toronto: Pearson Prentice Hall, pp. 266–294.

Engel, G. L., 1977. The need for a new medical model: A challenge for biomedicine. *Science*, 196(4286), pp. 129–136. http://dx.doi.org/10.1126/science.847460

Fishbein, M. and Ajzen, I., 1975. *Belief, attitude, intention, behaviour: An introduction to the theory and research*. Reading, MA: Addison-Wesley.

Foster, C., Hillsdon, M., Cavill, N., Allender, S. and Cowburn, G., 2005. *Understanding participation in sport: A systematic review*. London: Sport England.

Hausenblas, H. A., Carron, A. V. and Mack, D. E., 1997. Applications of the theories of reasoned action and planned behavior to exercise behavior, a meta-analysis. *Journal of Sport & Exercise Psychology*, 19(1), pp. 36–51.

Houlihan, B., 2000. Sporting excellence, schools and sports development: The politics of crowded policy spaces. *European Physical Education Review*, 6(2), pp. 171–193.

Houlihan, B. and White, A., 2002. *The politics of sport development: Development of sport or development through sport?* London: Routledge.

King, A. C., Stokols, D., Talen, E., Brassington, G. S. and Killingsworth, R., 2002. Theoretical approaches to the promotion of physical activity: Forging a transdisciplinary paradigm. *American Journal of Preventive Medicine*, 23(2S), pp. 15–25.

King, P., Dowling, E., Mueller, R., White, K., Schultz, W., Osborn, P., Dickerson, E., Bobek, D., Lerner, R., Benson, P. and Scales, P., 2005. Thriving in adolescence: The voices of youth serving practitioners, parents and early and late adolescents. *Journal of Early Adolescence*, 25(1), pp. 94–112.

Kirk, D. and Gorely, T., 2000. Challenging thinking about the relationship between school physical education and sport performance. *European Physical Education*, 6(2), pp. 119–134.

Kohl, H. W., Craig, C. L., Lambert, E. V., Inoue, S., Alkandari, J. R. and Leetongin, G., 2012. The pandemic of physical inactivity: Global action for public health. *The Lancet*, 380(9838), pp. 294–305. http://dx.doi.org/10.1016/S0140-6736(12)60898-8

Maslow, A. H., 1954. *Motivation and personality*. New York: Harper & Row.

Prochaska, J. O., Diclemente, C. C. and Norcross, J. C., 1992. In search of how people change: Applications to addictive behaviours. *American Psychologist*, 47(9), pp. 1102–1114.

Prochaska, J. O. and Velicer, W. F., 1997. The transtheoretical model of behavior change. *American Journal of Health Promotion*, 12(1), pp. 38–48.

Rittel, H. W. J. and Webber, M. M., 1973. Dilemmas in a general theory of planning. *Policy Sciences*, 4(2), pp. 155–169.

Scheerder, J., Vandermeerschen, H., Van Tuyckom, C., Hoekman, R., Breedveld, K. and Vos, S., 2011. *Understanding the game: Sport participation in Europe: Facts, reflections and recommendations*. Sports Policy and Management, 10. Leuven, Belgium: K.U. Leuven.

Scitovsky, T., 1992. *The joyless economy. The Psychology of Human Satisfaction*. Revised edition first published 1976. New York, Oxford: Oxford University Press.

Sirgy, M. J. and Wu, J., 2009. The pleasant life, the engaged life, and the meaningful lie: What about the balanced life? *Journal of Happiness Studies*, 10(2), pp. 183–196. http://dx.doi.org/10.1007/s10902-007-9074-1

Tay, L. and Diener, E., 2011. Needs and subjective well-being around the world. *Journal of Personality and Social Psychology*, 101(2), pp. 354–365.

United Nations, 1998. *Human development report 1998*. United Nations Development Programme. Oxford: Oxford University Press.

Chapter 5

Sport participation over the life-course

Linking the evidence to sporting capital theory

In this chapter I review the evidence on determinants of participation in sport across the life-course through the lens of sporting capital theory. In doing so I 'sense check' the theory and point towards the implications for policy and practice that flow from the new perspective it provides. This review is meant neither to be exhaustive nor definitive. The body of evidence and literature is wide and inevitably what is included here is selective. A lot of the evidence, particularly amongst the young, relates to determinants of 'physical activity' rather than to a narrow definition of sport, reflecting the wider academic interest and corpus of research in this area and the policy interest it attracts with its association to public health outcomes. For this I am unapologetic. Amongst the very young in particular, physical activity, the attitudes towards it and the basic motor skills associated with it are inextricably bound up with the predisposition to take part in sport. To return to a phrase used earlier, being physically active is a necessary if not always a sufficient condition for being a regular sustained participant in sport.

Although I have endeavoured to create a logical flow in the content of this book to make it readable for those who are prepared to invest the time and effort to progress through it from front page to back cover, there is an element of both reflective and prospective thinking in this chapter. To some extent the thinking that underpinned the development of my ideas on sporting capital are the accumulation of many years of 'on the job' experience of working at a strategic level in a national sports development agency as a 'bridge' between academic research and public policy administration. So inevitably some of the research evidence referred to may be considered as reflective in so far as it was influential, albeit quite often subliminally, in moulding and shaping my formative thinking until it coalesced into the theoretical proposition of sporting capital explained in Chapter 3. Importantly and additionally, however, in writing this book I have not only revisited research that I was previously familiar with but also made connections and followed new leads that have served to add evidential weight to the theory and its potential application. As a consequence this chapter has a central role in this book, both metaphorically and literally, as a retrospective connection back to the formulation of the theory and as contributing to a prospective debate on where the theory might take us both academically and practically in the future.

Because of the scope of this chapter it has not been an easy one to conceptualise and structure. The general theme is to take some of the key propositions that flow from the theory of sporting capital and explore what the evidence has to say that is relevant to those propositions. Central to the idea of sporting capital is the proposition that having more or less of it impacts not just on an individual's current probability of playing sport but also on the likely future prospects of sustaining participation into middle and older age. The orientation in this chapter, therefore, is to take a life-course approach to participation in sport, starting with what we know about the determinants of sport (and physical activity) in the very young, but importantly reviewing the evidence of how early experiences impact on and track through into adulthood. In the process I touch on the evidence for early socialisation into sport and the impact of parents and the family; the motivational climate particularly in school settings; and the importance of motor skill development and 'physical literacy' and its association with 'perceived competence'. The second part of the chapter goes on to examine what we know about adult determinants of participation, the barriers faced and the constraints and opportunities for re-engagement in sport amongst older people. Throughout, evidence of gender and social class differences in the determinants of participation are referenced, but again it should be made clear that although sensitive to these differences this review is far from comprehensive on this account.

Sport through the life-course

For most, if not all, sports participation starts when they are very young. Unfortunately for far too many, sports participation also stops when they are young. The ongoing public policy concern about early drop out from sport and policies prioritising young people was discussed in Chapter 2. To focus concern exclusively on early drop out is, however, to neglect the complexity of engagement or non engagement in sport throughout the life-course. Statistically sports participation peaks amongst the young and then declines with age (Rowe, Adams and Beasley, 2004; Van Bottenburg, Rijnen and van Sterkenburg, 2005). In most European countries participation in sport at a young age is significantly higher for boys than it is for girls; the exceptions being Denmark, the Netherlands, Sweden and Finland. But interestingly, with age the gap between the genders narrows (Van Tuyckom, Scheerder and Bracke, 2010; Apostolou, 2015). Figure 5.1 showing data from England provides a graphic demonstration of this drop out with age and gender after the age of 16 years. It also shows how even by the age of 16,

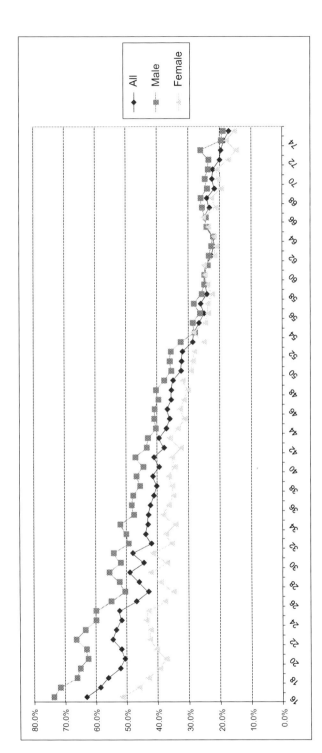

Figure 5.1 Participation rates in sport in England by age (16 plus) and gender. Participation is defined as at least once a week moderate intensity and at least 30 minutes' duration

Source: adapted from Sport England Active People Survey 2009/10 (APS4)

when sport involvement is still compulsory through the school PE curriculum, regular sports participation (at least once a week) in England is about 50 percent for young women and 75 percent for young men.

This traditional perspective on participation in sport, raising the spectre of early drop out, gender differences and declining participation with age, paints a picture that has important implications for public policy and its impact. However, the static cross sectional view of behaviour that it presents hides the dynamic temporal complexity of sport participation for any given individual over their life-course (Roberts et al., 1991). As a consequence, it provides a perspective that can be misleading (Birchwood, Roberts and Pollock, 2008; Rowe and Radford, 2010 unpublished), potentially taking public policy in the wrong direction to target interventions that are mismatched with the realities of people's relationship to sport at different points in their lives. The sport participation system, rather than static, should be thought of as in a continuous state of flux or 'churn'. A recent large-scale empirical longitudinal survey of participation behaviours in England (Matthews et al., 2016) showed that although the overall levels of sports participation remained stable, there was substantial change in the frequency of participation at the individual level; around two in five (41 percent) of respondents reported some change in their frequency of sport participation between their interview in year one and their interview in year three. This was equally split between increased participation (20 percent) and decreased participation (21 percent).

Change, flux, churn and volatility characterise all sporting behaviours across the life-course; they are the norm not the exception. Some people will be constant, regular sports participants throughout their lives but these are rare. The most committed sport enthusiast will have periods of illness or injury or will find themselves facing pressures of, for example family or work circumstances, that distract them from their 'sporty' routine (see Gershuny, 2003 for the impact of life transitions). In a systematic review of the evidence published between 1997 and 2007 Allender, Hutchinson and Foster (2008, p. 171) identified five broad areas of life events that impacted on individual's levels of physical activity: change in employment status; change in residence; change in physical status; change in relationships; and change in family structure. They did conclude, however, that they

> were surprised at the limited number of life events covered by this research. Potential areas for future study might include change from junior to secondary school and from secondary school to further and higher education (see Williamson et al., 1990 for evidence of increasing sedentary behaviours and weight increase for college students making the transition into the workplace); fatherhood; bereavement; and so on.
>
> (Allender, Hutchinson and Foster, 2008, p. 171)

The most sporty and active people will, even over a relatively short period of their lives, say one to three years, have periods when they are doing a lot of sport, periods when they are doing some sport but infrequently and periods when they are doing none. The extent of this flux is shown in Figures 5.2 and 5.3 where people were asked to retrospectively assess their participation status. It is interesting to note that the evidence suggests that levels of 'churn' are higher amongst the young than they are amongst the older population (see also Dovey, Reader and Chalmers, 1998). High levels of churn are inevitably associated with a higher risk of permanent or more sustained drop out, and this is what we see as many young people start to become more distanced from active participation in sport as they progress through adolescence and into adulthood in the face of competing pressures on their time and the growing attraction of other leisure choices.

The crucial consequence for public policy of this inherent instability in individual sporting behaviour is to dispense with the intuitively appealing but unrealistic aim of seeking to ensure that we create a population of regular *constant* participants and more realistically seek to ensure that: 1) people are more resilient to the life circumstances that get in the way of their sport and are inclined to stick with it even when they are challenging, in fact to even see sport as a way of ameliorating those challenges; and 2) when

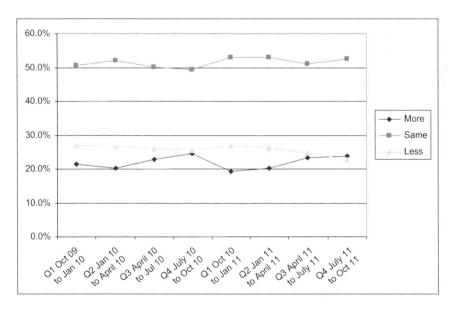

Figure 5.2 Changes in participation: percentages saying they are doing the same, more or less sport than at the same time last year by quarter

Source: adapted from Sport England Active People Survey, April 2009 to March 2011

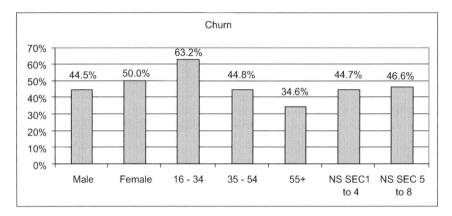

Figure 5.3 Percentage of adults doing either more or less sport than they did at the same time last year by gender, age and social class

Source: adapted from Sport England, Active People Survey, Jan to March 2011 (APS5)

inevitable drop out or 'participation reduction' occurs, to ensure that individuals are equipped with the stock of skills, psychological resources and social connections that provide them with the motivation and relatively easy route back into participation when circumstances become more favourable. Put another way, that is to have public policy that promotes participation in sport by creating the right environments, processes and mechanisms that build high levels of sporting capital across all groups in the population.

The early socialisation process – starting young

Many years of research and practitioner experience have contributed towards an extensive evidence base on the determinants of sporting behaviour at different stages in people's lives. It is not my intention in this chapter to attempt to systematically review that evidence base but instead to look for consistent themes that may be important in shaping the development and application of sporting capital theory to sport participation across the life-course. One clear theme that emerges from the research evidence that is consistent with what we would expect from sporting capital theory is the importance of the early socialisation process and its impact on later sports participation. Socialisation has been defined as "the process whereby individuals learn skills, traits, values, attitudes, norms, and knowledge associated with the performance of present or anticipated social roles" (McPherson and Brown, 1988, p. 267). Brustad (1992, p. 60) refers to three conceptual components that have traditionally defined the sport socialisation process,

Socialization *into* sport refers to the social and psychological influences that shape an individual's initial attraction to sport. . . . Socialization *via* sport refers to the acquisition of attitudes, values, and knowledge as a consequence of sport involvement. Socialization out of sport involves those influences that contribute to an individual discontinuing his or her sport participation.

The pervasiveness of sport in modern Western societies is a cultural phenomenon. Sport invades our consciousness from the youngest of ages; from the direct experience of taking part or watching family and friends take part to the secondary but no less powerful experiences associated with mass media images of elite sports teams, iconic individuals, mega events, advertising and consumption. Images of sport, its meanings, values, norms, expected behaviours, moral codes (or lack of them), gender stereotypes, body image, ways of dressing and use of language bombard young people daily and seep into their consciousness to impact on their perceptions of self and identity. It is not surprising, therefore, that sporting capital theory would suggest that early life experience is critical in shaping an individual's lifelong relationship to sport. This proposition is backed up by the evidence that places the impact of early socialisation processes on later sport participation as one of the dominant themes that emerges from the research literature.

As might be expected parents have been identified in the research as being a key influence on the sporting dispositions and identities of the very young (Baxter-Jones and Maffulli, 2003; Carson, 2016). Bandura's social learning theory (Bandura,1977) has been influential in contextualising and interpreting these parental influences with 'role modelling' of both attitude and behaviour thought to play an important part in the early socialisation process (Yang, Telama and Laakso, 1996; Wold and Anderssen, 1992). Research on the influence of parents on their children's sport and physical activity behaviours has not, however, been without debate over the relative influence of mothers and fathers and on the differential impact on the children themselves depending upon their gender. Some researchers have found the fathers to be more important (Lewko and Greendorfer, 1978; Yang, Telema and Laakso, 1996); some have concluded that the mothers' physical activity influences girls and is more confined to physical activity behaviours than it is to sport (McMurray et al., 1993); and others that the parents' physical activity behaviour only influences the same sex children, mothers to daughters and fathers to sons (Wold and Anderssen , 1992). A systematic review of the evidence on parental influences on different types and intensities of physical activity in youth (Edwardson and Gorely, 2010, p. 531) concluded that,

The cross-sectional findings . . . suggest that to facilitate activity for children aged 6–11 years, parents may need to be directly involved in participating in physical activity themselves. Furthermore, children who perceive their mother and/or father to be physically active are more likely to engage in physical activity. However, for children to engage in organised PA (physical activity) parents may need to provide broader support and facilitate their child's physical activity by encouraging their child to be active, transporting their child to places where she/he can be active as well as being active role models for their child.

The evidence supports the contention that an individual's relationship to sport is determined at a young age. By the time many, if not most young people leave secondary school their future prospects for taking part in sport as an adult have been shaped (Kirk, 2004; Vanreusel et al., 1997; Telama et al., 2006; Telama et al., 1997; Scheerder et al., 2005). Godin and Shephard (1986) have suggested that physical activity during childhood is vital to developing the positive attitudes that make such activities enjoyable, and to sustaining active lifestyles during adulthood. Tammelin et al. (2003) provide evidence that participation in sport-related activities as an adolescent is a strong indicator of physical activity into adulthood. Roberts et al. (1991) in their seminal work in the early 1990s looking at 'sporting careers' concluded that there is a heavy drop-out in youth and young adulthood, but people who remain sports-active throughout these life-stages are then most likely to remain active in sport for many more years. They go on to conclude that "long-term sport careers are usually built upon wide repertoires of interests and skills acquired early in life, and during such careers there is typically considerable mobility from sport to sport" (p. 261).

Roberts and Brodie (1992), found that the adults in their study who were continuous sports participants became 'bound-in' by their desire to repeat enjoyable experiences, to use their skills and to maintain the social relationships that they had built up. Côté et al. (2009) and Kirk (2005) also refer to the importance of a diversity of sporting experience; the 'sampling' of different sports at a young age. According to Côté et al. (2009), the significance of sampling for continued sports participation is its association with the development of social networks, 'which serve to bind individuals to sport', and the acquisition of fundamental motor skills, which are associated with self-perceptions of competence and, subsequently, to motivation (see the discussion later in this chapter). Birchwood, Roberts and Pollock (2008) go so far as to postulate, from evidence gained from their study in the Caucasus, that it is family culture that principally 'determines' an individual's enduring propensity to play sport. This is consistent with Bourdieu (1984), who views physical activity choices as socially structured reflecting possession and deployment of varying degrees of economic, cultural and symbolic capital. Birchwood, Roberts and Pollock (2008) make a direct link to Bourdieu stating that their evidence suggests that children acquire something akin to a Bourdieu type 'habitus', a set of 'deeply rooted predispositions' that is shaped by their social context and transmitted via socialisation in the family. This leads them to conclude that,

> This is not to suggest that participation rates remain unchanged from childhood onwards, which is clearly not the case. Life events make an impact, but how individuals respond can depend on their predispositions. Our evidence points to the family, and more specifically to the cultural dimension of family environments, as the prime source of these predispositions.
>
> (p. 296)

Stuij (2015) in her research on elementary school children in the Netherlands demonstrates how the socialisation process into sport is impacted by social class differences in the family with children from families of higher socio-economic groups being mainly influenced by the nuclear family and those from lower socio-economic groups learning in a 'less organised way' from the extended family network, friends and PE teachers. Dagkas and Stathi (2007) in a study of 16-year-old adolescents in the Midlands of England also found that the influence of their peers was greater among young people from lower socio-economic backgrounds than those from higher socio-economic groups. Duncan et al. (2002) reported that young people from lower economic strata experience greater barriers (e.g. financial, location, proximity of facilities) to activity than students from higher socio-economic status. They also, however, refer to the difference in levels of physical activity between high and low socio-economic status groups in their study potentially being the result of the habitus of these groups with those from lower socio-economic groups having a more instrumental view about the use of the body while those from higher socio-economic groups attaching higher value to body maintenance, health enhancing outcomes and the body as an end in itself. Children from high and low socio-economic status groups "would therefore hold differing levels of physical capital which would manifest itself in different levels of physical activity" (Duncan et al., p. 41).

The empirical evidence from research commissioned by Sport England (MORI, 2003) shows the level of drop out and disenchantment with sport particularly, but not solely, amongst girls that occurs in the teenage years. At the end of compulsory schooling many more girls than boys had a negative attitude to sport although general awareness of the benefits of an active lifestyle were high for both genders. In the MORI survey just over two in five (43 percent) pupils agreed that they *'prefer to do things other than sport and exercise in their free time'*, with 16 percent agreeing strongly. A preference for *'other'* activities was higher among girls than among boys (49 percent versus 36 percent). Among girls aged 11 years and above, interest in 'other' activities exceeded that for sport and exercise (51 percent).

This result was consistent with older girls' lower rates of participation in, and more negative attitudes towards sport. (Biddle et al., 2004).

Seeing oneself as a 'sporty type of person' may be considered as a proxy measure for sporting capital although further research is required to establish how much the two are correlated. Notwithstanding, it is interesting to examine the empirical data of self perception of 'sportiness' that was measured in the 2002 MORI survey of young people (MORI, 2003). The results, summarised in Figure 5.4, show that even by primary school age, girls are less likely to see themselves as a *'sporty type of person'* than boys (58 percent of boys agreeing strongly compared with 37 percent of girls). Self perceptions of how sporty they are decreases for both genders into secondary school age years, but the gender gap is maintained with 50 percent of boys agreeing strongly that they are a *'sporty type of person'* compared with 28 percent of girls. Perhaps of more concern is the nearly one in five girls (17 percent) who by the time they reach secondary school age *'disagree strongly'* that they are *'a sporty type of person'*. It is not surprising given the above statistics that when responding to the statement *'When I leave school I want to carry on doing sport and exercise'*, 29 percent of secondary age girls and 13 percent of boys responded negatively. The seeds of later life drop out have been sown. Evidence from research carried out by Horn et al. (2008) of young women transitioning from school to the first year 'post graduation' showed that girls who played sports in twelfth grade were 1.9 times more likely to be highly active one year post graduation. MORI (2003) used their 2002 data to create an interesting typology of young people based on their participation and attitudes towards sport which has clear resonance with the Sporting Capital Index presented later. Twenty-six percent of young people were classified as *'sporty types'* with a high propensity to take part in sport and very positive attitudes; 37 percent

I am a sporty type of person	Primary: Yrs 2-6			Secondary: Yrs 7-11			Total
	Boys	Girls	Total	Boys	Girls	Total	Yrs2-11
	%	%	%	%	%	%	%
Agree Strongly	58	37	47	50	28	39	43
Agree Slightly	23	29	26	25	27	26	26
Disagree Slightly	11	20	15	14	24	19	17
Disagree Strongly	5	10	8	7	17	12	10
Don't Know	3	4	4	6	4	5	4

Figure 5.4 Views about sport and leisure – how strongly agreed or disagreed with each statement, by whether primary or secondary, and sex (MORI, 2003)

as *'untapped potentials'* who like sport but have lower propensity to participate regularly; 14 percent characterised as *'unadventurous'* who don't mind sport but have a narrow range of sport participation interests; 24 percent as *'tolerators'* who dislike sport but still participate albeit reluctantly; and 9 percent as *'couch potatoes'* who dislike sport intensely with very low participation.

The early learning motivational climate

A second theme that is implicit in sporting capital theory is the nature of the learning environment and its impact on the psychological and physical determinants of participation in physical activity and sport. It has long been argued that positive experiences in PE could influence children to adopt physically active adult lifestyles which can improve public health (Sallis and McKenzie,1991; Shephard and Trudeau, 2000). There has been considerable research to better understand "the motivational, cognitive, and affective processes that can determine whether children will regard PE as a valuable, enjoyable, and rewarding experience, or as a worthless, boring, and humiliating one" (Ntoumanis, 2001, p. 226). There is evidence that students are more likely to want to continue their involvement in an activity if their PE lessons allow them to experience self-determination, and feel competent in their own abilities (Greenwood-Parr and Oslin, 1998). Self efficacy (Bandura, 1977, 1997), i.e. the extent or strength of one's belief in one's own ability to complete tasks and reach goals, has been shown in a number of studies to be significantly related to levels of physical activity in young people (Bungum et al., 2000; Garcia and King., 1991; Hagger, Chatzisarantis and Biddle, 2001).

Distinctions have been made between an intrinsically motivated learning environment, i.e. where there are no external rewards and the activity is undertaken because of interest in the activity itself; an extrinsically motivated approach where the activity is taken part in as a means to an end and not an end in itself; and what has been defined as 'amotivation' where individuals perceive no contingencies between outcomes and their actions and their dominant feeling are ones of incompetence and uncontrollability (Deci and Ryan, 1985). Biddle et al. (2011, p. 1) in their systematic review of '10 correlates of achievement goal orientations' found evidence that,

> A task orientation has a moderate-to-large association with the belief that effort causes success. Conversely, an ego orientation has a moderate-to-large association with the belief that ability causes success. In addition, a task orientation is associated with beliefs that the purposes of sport and physical education concern mastery/ co-operation, fitness/ health, and development of self-esteem. Ego orientation is associated with beliefs concerning the gaining of social status.

Ntoumanis (2001, p. 236) in his study of British students aged 14 to 16 years in the northwest of England found that,

> those with prior experience who feel and are physically competent are more likely to find PE interesting and fun, and want to participate in it to further develop their sport skills (i.e. they have self-determined motivation) . . . those who perceive that they lack physical competence usually find the PE experience meaningless (amotivation), and engage in it only because it is the rule or because of fear of punishment (external regulation).

This link between perceptions of competence and levels of activity has been shown to apply to sport, exercise and leisure-time physical activity in a range of different settings (Brustad, 1993; Luke and Sinclair, 1991; Telama, 1998; Taylor et al., 2010).

Research has shown that the intention to be physically active after leaving school was positively predicted by intrinsic motivation (Biddle et al., 1995; Pelletier et al., 1995; Ntoumanis, 2001). This has led Ntoumanis (2001, p. 238) to conclude that,

> Special attention should be given to those who feel pressured to participate or believe that they waste their time in PE. Usually, these students have low competence, find PE activities boring, and are the prime candidates for leading a sedentary life. Therefore, interventions should be developed to increase their perceived physical competence and intrinsic motivation toward PE.

In his study of 14 to 16-year-olds in 10 state schools in the northwest of England Ntoumanis (2002) found young people fell into three distinct groups according to a classification based on measures related to 'perceived mastery' and 'perceived performance'. One group made up of 44 percent of the students were self-determined and experienced positive affective and behavioural outcomes; another group, 42 percent of the sample, reported moderate levels of self-determination; and 14 percent indicated high levels of amotivation and external regulation accompanied by negative affective and behavioural outcomes. He suggested that these results although not overwhelmingly negative "signify that policy makers and PE teachers should have some cause for concern" (p. 192).

Research evidence makes a link between levels of enjoyment and likelihood of continuing to participate (Wankel, 1993). Weiss (1987) concludes that children will be more inclined to participate in physical activity if they perceive it to be enjoyable, and the chances of continued participation will be increased by enhancing their intrinsic motivation. Sallis et al. (1999, p. 413) in their research with 1,504 children in Grades 4–12 in the United States had findings that led them to suggest that "enjoyment of physical education classes should be considered a health-related goal because it is related to physical activity outside of school." Biddle et al. (2003) concluded that girls are less likely to enjoy and respond to competitive sport than boys and generally respond better to intrinsic (self improvement) rather than extrinsic (comparative performance with others) motivation. In a study of Estonian adolescents Viira and Raudsepp (2000) found that task orientation, effort and ability beliefs for males and cooperation, boredom and enjoyment for females were the most important correlates of moderate to vigorous physical activity participation. In a systematic review of the evidence related to adolescent girls participation in physical activity Biddle et al. (2005, p. 430) concluded that,

> The most extensive and consistent evidence suggests we should ensure that all physical activity environments for adolescent girls allow for choices and the development of perceptions of competence and confidence. This is likely to lead to higher levels of enjoyment, better physical self-worth, and stronger persistence.

The evidence that these factors relate differently to young men and women with an early socialisation process that leads to gender stereotyping is repeatedly shown in a number of studies (Cox, Coleman and Roker, 2006; Women's Sport and Fitness Foundation, 2012). Research has suggested that among adolescents and especially girls, the fear of being 'embarrassed' by poor performance or 'letting the team down' was a negative aspect of team sports (Mulvihill, Rivers and Aggleton, 2000; Coakley and White, 1992).

The evidence shows that body image can serve as both a motivator and a barrier to participation in sport and physical activity (Brudzynski and Ebben, 2010; Ingledew and Sullivan, 2002). Issues of body image and appearance seem to be important for adolescent girls and are negatively associated with physical activity (Biddle et al., 2011; Slater, 2011). Slater (2011, p. 461) in a study of adolescent boys and girls in South Australia found that,

> While playing sport girls were more likely to feel that people were staring at them because of how they looked, to be laughed at because of their appearance or for being uncoordinated, and to be called names that referred to their size or weight.

They concluded "that experiences of teasing and associated body image concerns may be contributing to the higher rates of withdrawal from physical activity observed around early adolescence in girls" (p. 462). Traditional notions of femininity and gender stereotyping impact particularly on young women's levels of physical activity as they transition into adulthood.

Duncan et al. (2004) found that, as school year increased, body esteem scores increased for boys but decreased for girls.

The evidence presented above is consistent with and supports the importance placed on the psychological domain in the theory of sporting capital. Building a 'stock' of positive dispositions around self identity, self confidence, self efficacy and body image is fundamental to whether a young person takes part in sport (Fox, 2000). Sporting capital theory suggests that socio-cultural norms have a significant impact on both the 'stock' of capital and on the experience of using that capital, i.e. in the nature of the participation experience. The evidence supports the proposition in sporting capital theory that early learning experiences have long-term consequences with positive or negative psychological attributes having a pervasive and durable impact on participation or drop out into adulthood. Sporting capital theory would suggest that for most, and particularly those with lower levels of sporting capital, an intrinsically motivated learning climate would be essential to sustain engagement and avoid disenchantment and drop out. This is particularly the case amongst girls but certainly not exclusively so.

The importance of fundamental movement skills

So far I have examined the evidence of the socialisation processes that impact on young people's participation in sport and how it tracks into adulthood. Many, however, consider fundamental motor skill mastery as a prerequisite to the development of more specific sports and physical activity related skills (Ulrich, 1987; Wickstrom, 1983). Whitehead (2010, p. 5) has stressed the importance of the wider concept of physical literacy defined as, "the motivation, competence, knowledge and understanding that individuals develop in order to maintain physical activity at an appropriate level throughout their life." In Whitehead's definition physical literacy encompasses far more than physical education in schools or structured sporting activities although her ideas have been embraced by and had important implications for both (Lundvall, 2015). Whitehead (2010, p. 7) defines an individual who is physically illiterate as someone who

> will have no confidence in their ability in the field of physical activity anticipating no rewarding feedback from such involvement. Individuals will have a very low level of self esteem with respect to this aspect of their potential and will avoid all inessential physical activity in order to guard against failure and humiliation.

This is not a recent phenomenon. In the early1990s Coakley and White (1992) found that lack of competence was one of the most negative experiences reported by girls in PE.

Taking a narrower perspective, Stodden et al. (2008) have argued that the development of motor skills or 'fundamental movement skills' is an important but often overlooked precursor to greater perceived physical competence and future physical activity participation. Writing in 2008, Stodden suggested that,

> Current literature in physical activity generally has not focused on the developmental nature of motor skill competence and its role in promoting physical activity across time. In essence, investigators have focused on measuring physical activity in children without an understanding that learning to move is a necessary skill underlying physical activity.
>
> (Stodden et al., 2008, p. 291)

It has been suggested that children who participate in sport and achieve greater levels of motor skill competence during childhood and adolescence will remain active participants in physical activity into adulthood (Malina, 1996). Wrotniak et al. (2006), examining the relationship in 8 to 10-year-old children of motor skill competence and children's self-perceptions of adequacy, found motor skill competence was positively associated with physical activity and perceptions of adequacy in performing and inversely associated with sedentary activity.

Stodden et al. (2008, p. 291) suggest that, "if children cannot proficiently run, jump, catch, throw, etc., then they will have limited opportunities for engagement in physical activities later in their lives because they will not have the prerequisite skills to be active." They go on to refer to a 'physical activity divide' that occurs between childhood and adolescence with, in one group low-skilled, inactive children who perceive themselves as poorly skilled, and in the other group their higher skilled, more active counterparts who find physical activity rewarding. The evidence shows, however, that considering socio-cultural processes and physical development processes as separate and independent is a gross oversimplification. For example Barnett et al. (2010) found more boys in their study performed object control skills (kick, throw or catch) proficiently than girls and that childhood object control proficiency influenced proficiency in adolescence. They conclude that "One explanation for these findings is that boys may receive greater encouragement, positive reinforcement, and prompting to participate in activities involving object control skills, particularly throughout adolescence" (p. 167). Wilkinson, Littlefair and Barlow-Meade (2013, p. 161) in a review of the published evidence conclude that,

> socially privileged definitions of the good student that serve to narrow interpretations of ability within the school PE environment operate to enhance the achievement possibilities of only a few, mostly male, students, whose abilities approximate the dominant values of the field.

The importance of interpersonal relationships – socialisation beyond the family

As important as the physical and psychological domains are to levels of sporting capital, the interpersonal dimension of sport participation should not be underrated. Sport participation takes place within a network of social relationships; very rarely if ever is participation in sport a completely solitary activity. These social relationships or connections frame, facilitate and enable participation and equally can frustrate, limit and increase the likelihood of non engagement or drop out when they break down or fail to become established. People seek out relationships that support and nurture their interests and in turn those interests extend and build the social networks and connections that reinforce participation (Kyle and Chick, 2004). Opportunities to engage in social networks and be part of social recreational experiences and activities have been found to be important drivers of sustained leisure activity involvement (e.g. Kyle et al., 2007; Wood and Danylchuk, 2011). The increasing influence of peers on identity formation occurs as young people move into adolescence when they are often adopting the behaviours, values and beliefs common to the group in which they have chosen to belong (Newman and Newman, 1995).

Research by Smith (1999, p. 346) highlighted the important influence friends have on adolescents' attraction to sports and games, physical exertion and vigorous exercise leading them to conclude that,

> perceptions of both friendship and peer acceptance in physical activity settings can contribute to the formation of physical activity attitudes and behaviours of young adolescents. Thus, enhancing peer relationships in the physical activity setting might be a viable approach to promoting active living among young people.

Qualitative research on 15 to 19-year-old young women carried out by Coleman, Cox and Roker (2008) explored social influences, such as the role of friends and family upon contrasting levels of physical activity participation amongst young women who *always participate* in sport compared with those *who never participate*. They found that the vast majority of young women who always participated highlighted the positive impact that others have in influencing their activities and how they felt that their social life in particular supported their current level of sport participation. In contrast the vast majority of young women who never participated in physical activity felt their social life significantly restricted their option to participate. Although the role of the family was deemed to be a highly significant social influence (as discussed earlier), their research led them to conclude that the influence of friends was particularly strong for this group, such that:

it is reasonable to presume that psychological, individual-based factors may predispose a young women's likelihood to engage in high levels of physical activity; however, it is the influence of the family and friends which has a more significant influence on participation levels. The case studies extend this analysis by emphasizing the primary influence of the friendship group over that of the family on occasions.

(Coleman, Cox and Roker, p. 644)

Weiss and Smith (2002, p. 433) studying friendship quality amongst young tennis players found that, "junior tennis players who rated their best tennis friendship higher in similar beliefs and interests, companionship and pleasant play, and conflict resolution found their experiences more fun and pleasurable, and felt psychologically committed to continue their involvement in tennis." Wankel and Kreisel (1985, p. 63) in their study of factors underlying enjoyment in youth sports found that,

> A key consideration for providing an enjoyable sport experience would appear to be the grouping of participants into appropriate skill categories. Each child should be provided an opportunity to develop his or her skills, be provided with a reasonable challenge, and be afforded an opportunity for personal accomplishment and satisfaction.

Burch (1969), taking a sociological perspective, suggests that the origins of leisure participation and continued involvement are more often influenced by 'the social circles of workmates, family and friends' than by individual causes, i.e. by what he terms the 'personal community' hypothesis of leisure. The formation of social networks based on common leisure interests has been referred by Scott and Godbey (1992, p. 49) as 'social worlds' that

> represent a unique scheme of life in which members share in a special set of meanings . . . and in which various cultural elements – activities and events . . . conventions and practices . . . are created and made meaningful by social world members and serve to set the social world apart from other social worlds.

Previous research regarding positive youth development has recognised the developmental significance of sport peer groups (Holt and Jones, 2008) and the potential for positive and/or negative psychosocial experiences through sport involvement (Eccles et al., 2003; Fraser-Thomas and Côté, 2009) that can impact on an individual's choice to remain involved in sport (Fraser-Thomas, Côté and Deakin, 2005).

In Kyle and Chick's (2004, p. 253) study exploring the properties of enduring leisure involvement from the perspective of campers attending an agricultural encampment and fair in the United States, a number of major themes emerged explaining the enduring involvement of participants:

> (a) affirmation of family and friends, which referred to leisure contexts that supported ties to family and friends; (b) satisfaction with family and friends, which referred to the satisfaction derived from shared leisure experiences; (c) development of children, which referred to leisure contexts that permitted opportunities for parents to model their children's values and impart their own sense of morality; (d) development and maintenance of relationships, which referred to contexts that enabled informants to spend time with friends or make new friends; (e) interaction with others, which referred to leisure contexts that positively influenced informants' affect which, in turn, effected their interactions with those around them; and (f) location, which refers to the 'container' or settings in which informants' experiences occurred.

Kyle and Chick's research provides a wider leisure context which can be inferred to have implications for sport behaviour. However, Widdop, Cutts and Jarvie (2016, p. 597), taking a narrower focus, suggest that,

> little attention has been paid to how resources embedded in social networks – as measured by an individual's position in the social structure, diversity and homophily of an individual's network and the strength of ties in the network – influence sport participation.

The importance of the influence of these social networks on an individual's sporting behaviours is elaborated as follows,

> An individual may consume or play sport on their own but inevitably they interact, communicate and consume physical forms of sport with family, friends and acquaintances. Therefore, as well as diverse networks, who you share sports with socially will be important; the types of ties in your social networks will mediate participation behaviours. For example, sharing time with a diverse friendship network might be very different to having a diverse family network.
>
> (Widdop, Cutts and Jarvie, p. 602)

In their empirical study of adult participation in England, Widdop, Cutts and Jarvie (2016) identify four 'sport clusters'. The lowest populated group (7 percent) is labelled the *'highbrow omnivores'* who are distinguished from the other classes for their 'extremely active participation and sheer insatiable appetite for all the sporting items' including what are defined as 'highbrow sports' such as 'water sports, racket sports' and recreational sports. The next group is defined as the *'lowbrow omnivores'* (10 percent of the population) who are similar in many ways to their highbrow equivalents except insofar as they are light consumers of those sports traditionally deemed as status-defining sports (highbrow) and instead have a high participation rate in association football. The remaining two classes *'fitness class group'* (41 percent) and *'inactives'* (42 percent) have more restricted participation patterns, but make up 83 percent of the survey population. The fitness class group, which has a high prevalence of women, has relatively low participation in team and highbrow sports, and a high prevalence when they do participate in those sports most associated with health and body fitness. The *'inactives'* are differentiated from the other classes through their disengagement with sport. Of particular interest in this context is the extent of the social networks that characterise each group,

> Even when controlling for socio-demographic characteristics, both the 'highbrow omnivores' and 'lowbrow omnivores' are more likely to have a larger friendship network than the 'fitness class' and the 'non participants' have a much more restricted network, which reinforces their lack of partaking in sporting activities.
>
> (p. 612)

Barriers and constraints – the context for participation

As we have already seen, barriers and constraints to participation are the context in which sporting capital is expressed and impact on the propensity to take part in sport. The level of sporting capital an individual holds impacts on both her or his perceptions of barriers and their resilience to them (see Chapter 3). Sporting capital theory makes a distinction between intrapersonal (those embedded in the person), interpersonal (those that are defined by an individual's relationships) and structural or external constraints and barriers (those outside and independent of the individual and their social networks). Intra and interpersonal constraints are embedded in sporting capital theory in the psychological, physical and social domains. External constraints operate as mediating factors that "intervene between preference and participation" (Casper et al., 2011, p. S33) such as unavailability of resources required to participate (e.g. money, time, problems with facilities and social/geographical isolation). In a survey commissioned by Eurostat across 28 European Union member states (Eurostat, 2014), shortage of time was by far the main reason given for not practising sport more regularly (42 percent) with lack of motivation or interest mentioned by 20 percent, having a disability or illness by 13 percent or that it was too expensive by 10 percent. As with adults, adolescents often cite (lack of) time as the primary constraint although this has multiple meanings, and varies across cultures and by individuals (see

Godbey, 2005; Casper et al., 2011); the availability of partners (or lack of partners), an interpersonal barrier, was the second highest constraint found by Casper and colleagues in their study of adolescent participation in sport followed by the quality or crowdedness of available facilities (an external constraint). Physical activity, especially for children and adolescents, has been positively associated with accessible and convenient facilities (Hume, Salmon and Ball, 2005; Sallis et al., 2001).

The difference between objective and perceived constraints is an important one. Casper et al. (2011) found that while constraints to adolescent sport participation opportunities may be equal, the girls viewed constraints as more of a limiting factor toward continued participation than did the boys. They reference other sources which suggest that this may be partially explained by the notion that girls are perceived to have more restrictions due to household tasks and family responsibility, lower confidence and self esteem in physical activity/sport activities, and less social approval. All these factors are consistent with what would be predicted by sporting capital theory. A longitudinal study of 18 to 27-year-old women in Australia (Bell and Lee, 2005) found that the adoption of a traditionally feminine life path of marriage, motherhood and working unpaid in the home is associated with reductions in physical activity. Interestingly, their study also found that moving from a cohabiting relationship to a marriage was also associated with reductions in physical activity suggesting, "that (the) nature of the relationship affects women's physical activity, even if there is little change in actual living conditions, and supports the view that adoption of a more traditionally feminine lifestyle drives lower involvement in physical activity" (p. 233).

Flintoff and Scraton, writing in 2001 and taking a more general perspective about the reasons why girls are turned off from PE and sport, opened their article with the observation that,

> What is interesting about the latest research findings is their suggestion of 'new' evidence and concerns, and yet, in reality, the findings differ little from the information gathered in the 1980s. In many of the recent studies, girls continue to be viewed as a 'problem' for not engaging positively in PE, and the reasons cited by the girls remain remarkably similar to those from yesteryear – the wearing of PE uniform; the no-jewellery rules; compulsory showers; and having to play games outside in the cold.
>
> (p. 5)

Hills (2007, p. 318) suggests that the, "particular interest in relation to girls has been the relationship between physical education and identified areas of concern for young women such as developing bodies, appearance, health, sexuality, freedom, independence and control." Drawing evidence from their qualitative research with 15-year-old young women, Flintoff and Scraton (2001), however, challenged a dominant view which presented a picture of girls being 'switched off' to physical activity. To the contrary they concluded from their research that many young women enjoyed and were involved in physical activity, both in and out of school. They found that,

> the young women in our research were clearly influenced by dominant discourses of health and well being, seeing health benefits as a key purpose for taking part in physical activity. Physical activity also offered opportunities to be social with friends and the chance to learn new skills. However, in contrast the purpose of school PE was less clear. At best it was seen as a break from academic work; at worse, an unnecessary imposition impacting negatively on their academic studies, and one in which they rarely learned new skills useful for their out of school lives.
>
> (p. 11)

In 2008 Sport England commissioned the Henley Centre to carry out qualitative research focused on people who regularly play sport and the experiences that reinforce or potentially could lead them to drop out (Goretzki and Esser, 2008). The main findings from this research (also reported in Rowe, 2012) demonstrated that the quality of experience of sport was made up of a complex interaction of the personal, interpersonal and contextual as follows:

- The components of the good experience feel very consistent across sports. Differences between them are nuanced and a matter of weight – rather than fundamental.
- What makes a satisfying/'great' sport experience is far less about conditions (facilities, infrastructure and access) than subjective, emotional factors (how you are playing and how you feel).
- Performance – while relevant for all – is a more overt component of experience for organised sport versus informal play with the social element more salient for team sports compared with 'solo' sports.
- Performance is the emotional satisfaction of having played 'well' and put in credible effort, that is, having achieved potential. Potential is often expressed in terms of 'having performed to the standards I'm capable of'.
- 'Enjoying yourself' is the prime criterion for all sustained activity – and sits at the apex of any list of components. This said, it merely answers a question with another.
- The positive experience within often means feeling that you have 'put in some physical exertion'.

- Positive experiences are very likely to involve feeling that 'I'm getting a break from the everyday things in life'. This includes feeling diverted – escapism and focusing on other things.
- Sport's 'sociable' dimension is a recurring emotional component. Feeling included or accepted is an indicator of satisfaction with communal/team sports – but less of an issue for solo sports.
- 'Functional' drivers such as 'customer service' (staff attitudes, knowledge and ability), 'hygiene factors' (quality of showers, changing rooms, pool water and toilets), organisation and coaching emerge when we explore what can occasionally go 'wrong'. In many ways, these feel like 'hygiene factors' – without which a sporting target would simply 'walk away' after time.
- Good organisation/coordination is a feature of a positive experience in organised team sports

An ageing population – sport participation into older age

I have focused a lot of attention on young people's experience of sport and the factors that shape their early learning, socialisation, identity formation and its impact on their disposition towards sport through their life-course. However, it is important with an ageing population and what historically has seemed to be an inevitable drop out in participation in sport with age that public policy does not neglect this demographic. In 2011, 9.2 million (16 percent) of the usual residents of England and Wales were aged 65 and over, an increase of almost one million from 2001 (8.3 million or 16 percent) (Office for National Statistics, (ONS), 2013) and this trend is set to continue. Statisticians now tell us that life expectancy is rising by around five hours a day, or nearly three months each year (Kirkwood, 2006). A report published by NESTA (Khan, 2013, p. 5), drawing its title from the above statistic, states that

> one rule of thumb suggests that we should think of our chronological age as equivalent to a decade younger in our parents' lives. Today's 60 year old may be thinking and feeling more like a 50 year old a generation ago. Longer lives mean many more opportunities to live, to learn and to enjoy, and an end to the 20th century's vice of what Michael Young called 'chronologism': the assumption that education, work and retirement should all be prescribed according to our chronological age.

Long in his review paper commissioned by Sport England (Long, 2004, p. 35) made his views clear on 'ageism in sport policy' (my phrase, not his),

> Take the matter seriously – the message is clear and should provide a wake-up call for Sport England and the sporting community generally.

Such a large (and growing) part of the population . . . cannot be left out of the reckoning if Sport England is serious about substantially increasing the nations participant levels.

As we have seen earlier, sporting capital theory predicts that the probability of returning to sport in the later years is much higher for someone who has built up their stock of sporting capital in their youth compared with someone whose 'peak sporting capital' was low. The theory would suggest that the longer the span of non participation, the more opportunity there is for sporting capital to decrease through what might be considered a slow process of attrition. However, unless there is a life-changing event, particularly as it relates to an individual's health, then the decline in sporting capital will be gradual to the point that someone with high sporting capital in their youth will in their 50s and 60s still be likely to see themselves as 'sporty', may retain confidence in their sports-related physical skills and will continue to feel familiar with and not intimidated by the social norms and conventions that characterise sporting environments and situations. So investment in building sporting capital in the young is also an investment in the future by facilitating a return to sport amongst the older population when perhaps life circumstances change such as when leisure time increases with retirement.

Notwithstanding the benefits of investing in early positive experiences to build sporting capital, there is, however, a strong argument to suggest that: 1) the route back into sport for older age groups must be made as easy as possible; and 2) that although it poses particular challenges, it is never too late to build or rebuild sporting capital after a long 'layoff'. While the motivation to re-engage in sport in older age is influenced significantly by health and social drivers (Arkenford Ltd, 2006), interestingly, Schutzer and Graves (2004) quoted in Berlin and Klenosky (2014) found that the majority of research points to self efficacy as a critical factor in the decision of older people to begin an exercise routine. They found that self efficacy would then influence which activity an individual chooses, how much effort to expend, and the degree of persistence an individual devotes to the activity when faced with barriers. Grant (2001) found that older individuals participate in sports-based leisure for reasons other than health: to give life purpose, as a distraction from body pain, to escape from problems, to engage socially and to have fun. Other research suggests that "one's motivation to engage in an activity (e.g. enjoyment of the activity, being outdoors, enjoying the feel of water when swimming) may be a more important predictor of continued engagement than the health benefits of the activity itself" (Berlin and Klenosky, 2014 p. 128). In the same article examining older women's motivations for participation in sport Berlin and Klenosky (2014) refer to the importance of the challenge that participation in sport creates in relation to 'measuring results', 'satisfaction conquering a skill', 'engaging the mind', 'shows me that I am still capable' and 'know I am better at something'. For them this validates Wearing's (1995, p. 272) statement that "leisure emphasizes what a person can do rather than what they are no longer physically capable of doing." For Berlin and Klenosky (2014, p. 147), "This focus on success and results lead to the highly abstract values of *enrichment* and the *feelings of achievement.*"

Long (2004) proposed a number of ingredients to public policy if we are to boost participation rates in sport amongst the older population. The first was 'to maximise continuity' by which he referred to the need to keep those currently engaged involved in sport, "Sports bodies need to ensure there is always an alternative to let people continue in a different capacity or at a different intensity" (p. 35). This could include for example modified sports, veterans' leagues, or low intensity fitness activities. The second was to 'differentiate' both older people and sports/physical activities. That is, not to treat all older people as a homogenous group and to see different sports offering different benefits to different people. The third was to 'seek balance' by promoting "a different kind of sport that starts with the needs of the individual rather than an emphasis on training, competition, development of skills and ladder of progression" (p. 35). In my terms all three arguments support the case for matching the challenge and experience of sport to an individual's level of sporting capital. And finally Long implores sport policy makers and practitioners to 'don't go it alone', stressing the importance of public policy intervention in sport being integrated both horizontally and vertically with other agencies outside of sport that are more familiar with the challenges and opportunities of working with this (older) age group.

Summary and conclusions

This chapter has been wide ranging and it is important to draw the threads together to weave them back to the ideas, propositions and concepts of sporting capital theory introduced in Chapter 3. Key messages emerging from this chapter include:

- It is important to take a life-course perspective on participation in sport. Change, flux, churn and volatility characterise all sporting behaviours across the life-course; they are the norm not the exception. Too many people drop out of sport at a young age, never to return and too many of those who do return do so only briefly or spasmodically and fail to embed sport as an integral part of their lives.
- Transitions through the life-course impact on individuals' participation in sport and their more general activity levels. The change of environment of moving from primary to secondary school mixed up with the process of maturation and identity formulation that happens during

adolescence makes this a potentially fragile and certainly formative time in shaping an individual's relationship to sport. Later life events such as leaving school to go into the workplace or into further or higher education; change in employment status; change in residence; change in health and physical status; change in relationships; change in family structure and retiring from full time work all impact on sports participation, more often negatively than positively.

- Early learning experiences are critical in their influence on people's later life relationship to sport. Evidence that physical activity during childhood is vital to developing the positive attitudes that make such activities enjoyable and to sustaining active lifestyles during adulthood is strong. As might be expected, parents have been identified in the research as being a key influence on the sporting dispositions and identities of the very young. As young people get older, their range of influences broadens to include school and their peers as they transition into adolescence. By the time many, if not most young people leave secondary school, their future prospects for taking part in sport as an adult have been shaped if not defined.

- Most if not all young people take part in sport in school PE lessons. It has long been argued that positive experiences in PE could influence children to adopt physically active adult lifestyles which can improve public health. There is extensive evidence that an intrinsic motivational climate both in the school PE and family setting that emphasises mastery and self referenced goal setting and improvement over extrinsic external referenced comparative performance is associated with individual motivation for sustained commitment to sport. The evidence suggests that a wide diversity or 'sampling' of different sports at a young age impacts on the propensity to participate in later life. Direct evidence of school PE positively impacting on sport participation levels in later life is, however, at best equivocal with examples of both positive and negative experiences and practice. Most, however, would see school PE delivered in the right way, sensitive to the socio-psychological needs of the individual and to the cultural contexts that influence them as providing an important window of opportunity to influence and shape long-term disposition to sport and a physically active lifestyle.

- Psychological factors around self efficacy (a 'can do' attitude), self-determination (i.e. some control over what you do and why), identity (seeing yourself as 'sporty') and perceptions of competence (an able to do attitude) emerge as important influences on young people's participation. These factors are linked to enjoyment which has been identified in the research as the key to sustained commitment to an active and sporty lifestyle. A sense of 'physical self-worth' and gender stereotypes around body image and cultural expectations of femininity impact on girls' participation and attitudes towards sport and pose particular challenges that can increase drop out during the formative teenage years.

- Although psychological factors are important, it has been argued that attention to basic physical skill development has not received the prominence that it should in sport policy and pedagogy. It has been suggested that children who participate in sport and achieve greater levels of motor skill competence during childhood and adolescence will remain active participants in physical activity into adulthood. Actual motor skill development has been shown to be related to perceived competence which in turn predicts sustained participation. However, the evidence shows an expected complex interaction between psychological, socio-cultural and physical factors in shaping an individual's sporting identity and predisposition to take part in sport.

- As important as the physical and psychological domains are to levels of sporting capital, the interpersonal dimension of sport participation should not be underrated. Social connections – whether in the family, amongst peers or with significant others such as teachers, coaches and community workers – frame and impact on an individual's propensity to participate in sport. Social connections can be reinforcing, a kind of social glue that sustains involvement in sport. However, more negatively, they can operate as diversions from or active barriers to participation when the norms of the group are antipathetic to sport or an active lifestyle. During adolescence in particular, there are great pressures to conform, and although people young and old tend to gravitate towards the groups that are best aligned with their own preferences and predilections, this inclination does not always prevail. In time social networks themselves become reinforcing and the associated conforming behaviours should they be negative ones become ingrained and difficult to break away from even if the motivation is there to do so.

- Participation in sport is mediated or prevented by barriers and constraints. Opportunities may be thought of as the obverse side of a constraint. Understanding barriers and their distinctive nature is important. Barriers to participation in sport take three forms: intrapersonal, interpersonal and structural or 'external' constraints. Intrapersonal barriers are embedded in the person in the form of psychological or physical factors, while interpersonal barriers are those that relate to a person's social environment, the people with whom they mix and interact. Both of these types of barriers are integrated within and are part of sporting capital. External or structural constraints are those that are separate from the individual and can take a number of forms from the physical environment including topography, climate, urban structure, number and quality of facilities and their accessibility, to the economic environment including cost (both actual and opportunity cost associated with other demands on time), work demands and socio-cultural in terms of for example family responsibilities, including childcare and social care of the elderly or disabled. External barriers are relative. What might be perceived as a barrier to one person may be invisible to another or even viewed as an incentive or motivation to someone else.

- It is important with an ageing population and what historically has seemed to be an inevitable drop out in participation in sport with age that public policy does not neglect this demographic. Although there are strong arguments for intervention at a young age to build physical competency, positive psychological affect and positive social connections around sport, with an ageing population public policy cannot afford to neglect a more remedial approach to re-engaging those who have dropped out of sport in their youth or early middle age. Although health features increasingly as a prominent issue into older age, the research evidence suggests that a focus on health outcomes as a primary motivator for this group to participate in sport is a misplaced one. Research has shown that many older people engage in sports-based leisure for reasons other than health: to give life purpose, as a distraction from body pain, to escape from problems, to engage socially and to have fun. It has been argued that sport for older people should be about challenge, satisfaction in conquering a new skill, engaging the mind and with a focus on what an older person can do and not on what they are no longer physically capable of doing. This perspective on sport in older age is one of enriching life rather than focusing principally on a medical deficit model that sees sport as an intervention designed to deliver a dosage of threshold levels of exertion to prevent illness and physical deterioration.

Much of what is referred to above is consistent with the view of Weiss (2013, p. 564), who, reflecting on 25 years of psychological research on youth physical activity motivation, concluded that,

> Consistent with theory, robust findings exist for the three major "ingredients" of physical activity motivation. Findings repeatedly show that: (a) perceived competence is a strong predictor of self-determined motivation and physical activity level; (b) enjoyment is a powerful source of physical activity motivation and sustained participation; and (c) parents, coaches, and peers exhibit beliefs and behaviors that influence whether youth choose to be involved, how invested they are in physical activity, and what psychosocial and behavioral outcomes are attained as a consequence of participation.

These dimensions resonate with, if not mapping precisely, the three domains of sporting capital theory, the physiological, psychological and social.

Consistent with the evidence referred to in this chapter, sporting capital theory recognises the significance of physical literacy and fundamental movement skills in its formulation. It includes a physiological domain that encompasses both physical literacy and wider aspects of physical health. This is not to suggest, however, that the 'physical' is distinct and separable from the 'psychological' and even the social dimensions. Although the three domains are separated in the practical application and measurement process that identifies an individual's level of sporting capital, the reality is a complex interaction and synthesis of all three of these domains both in the building of sporting capital and in its expression through participation. This complex interaction of the social, psychological and physiological worlds is the lived reality of sport. To create silos around each is to misunderstand the very essence of what sport is about and if translated into a simplified view of public policy, intervention will almost certainly result in failure. The evidence in this review is clear: physical ability is inextricably mixed up with aspects of individual psychology related to identity, self confidence and self efficacy and people express their physicality in a social world that is framed by interpersonal relationships that are associated with status and recognition. All of this is in turn framed and influenced by the wider socio-cultural context of class, gender and associated power relationships within a society.

Sporting capital is a positive theory driven by a normative belief that something can be done to improve things. Albeit I fully accept the selective nature of the process, there is nothing presented in this scan of the evidence that would contradict the propositions made in sporting capital theory and much that would add weight and support to it. I acknowledge the epistemological argument for unconscious bias stemming from my starting position from which some things become salient and others might merge into the background. I can, however, vouch for the fact that nothing has been purposely omitted from my review of evidence because it had dissonance with the theoretical propositions of sporting capital, but inevitably some areas will be more contentious and less definitive than others as is the nature of social science and behaviour studies. On this count I refer back to what I said in Chapter 1 that 'my hope is that those in the academic world pick up the gauntlet to establish an evidence base that challenges and builds the theory in the contexts and disciplines in which their expertise lies, and ideally in multi-disciplinary and collaborative research frameworks'. The evidence presented in this chapter emphasises the importance of early formative experiences which is consistent with what we would expect from sporting capital theory. The development of physical competence, both actual and perceived, impacts not only on the immediate experiences and commitment of young people to active and sporty lifestyles, but extends to a lifelong predisposition towards or against these behaviours. The psychological dimensions of identity, physical self confidence and self efficacy emerge from the research evidence as critical in determining an individual's predisposition to take part in sport and again are characteristics that are shaped at an early age but with potentially long-lasting consequences. It is this long-lasting impact or what we might call 'tracking' of behaviour over the life-course that is connected to the idea of durability that is a key proposition in sporting capital theory, i.e. that sporting capital built at a young age has durability through the life-course. So while participation is subject to short term flux and change, sporting capital is sustained and like 'money in the bank' it can be drawn out a later date when circumstances are more favourable or require it. However, unlike money in the bank, it does not dwindle with use but given the right conditions increases the more you draw upon it.

The evidence points towards certain intervention styles that can be more effective, including an intrinsic motivation climate that emphasises mastery rather than comparative performance, a matching of the challenge to the skill and competency level, and a recognition of the importance of family and peers and of the social networks that can either promote or undermine sport participation and active lifestyles. All these themes are consistent with sporting capital theory. It highlights the socio-cultural context that permeates all sporting experiences most notably affecting gender and class relationships to sport. It shows that the barriers to sport are not simply ones of opportunity, albeit these do exist, but are more likely to be found in the intrapersonal and interpersonal worlds that people inhabit and that shape their psychosocial and ecological relationship to sport. In addressing these barriers we must look at both how sport needs to change in the way that it presents itself to people and at what we can change in people, i.e. their level of sporting capital to influence how they perceive and experience their external world in terms of what sport has to offer them. Cutting through this complexity, all roads lead back to one simple word, 'enjoyment'. Enjoyment lies at the heart of sport. Enjoyment is linked to experience and experience is linked to capability defined both physically and beyond the physical to include the psychological and social. Sporting capital empowers people to enjoy sport and to make it a central and fulfilling part of their lives. In the next chapter I move from an evidential review to empirical testing by presenting a way to operationalise and measure levels of sporting capital and through primary research to explore its relationship to participation and its prevalence in the English population.

References

Allender, S., Hutchinson, L. and Foster, C., 2008. Life-change events and participation in physical activity: A systematic review. *Health Promotion International*, 23(2), pp. 160–172.

Apostolou, M., 2015. The evolution of sports: Age-cohort effects in sports participation. *International Journal of Sport and Exercise Psychology*, 13(4), pp. 359–370. http://dx.doi.org/10.1080/1612197X.2014.982678

Arkenford Ltd., 2006. *Understanding participation in sport: What determines sports participation among recently retired people?* London: Sport England.

Bandura, A., 1977. *Social learning theory.* Englewood Cliffs, NJ: Prentice-Hall.

Bandura, A., 1997. *Self-efficacy: The exercise of control.* New York: W. H. Freeman.

Barnett, L. M., van Beurden, E., Morgan, P. J., Brooks, L. O. and Beard, J. R., 2010. Gender differences in motor skill proficiency from childhood to adolescence. *Research Quarterly for Exercise and Sport,* 81(2), pp. 162–170. http://dx.doi.org/10.1080/02701367.2010.10599663

Baxter-Jones, A. D. and Maffulli, N., 2003. Parental influence on sport participation in elite young athletes. *Journal of Sports Medicine and Physical Fitness,* 43(2), pp. 250–255.

Bell, S. and Lee, C., 2005. Emerging adulthood and patterns of physical activity among young Australian women. *International Journal of Behavioral Medicine,* 12(4), pp. 227–235.

Berlin, K. L. and Klenosky, D. B., 2014. Let me play, not exercise! A laddering study of older women's motivations for continued engagement in sports–based versus exercise–based leisure time physical activities. *Journal of Leisure Research,* 46(2), pp. 127–152.

Biddle, S. J. H., Atkin, A. J., Cavill, N. and Foster, C., 2011. Correlates of physical activity in youth: A review of quantitative systematic review. *International Review of Sport and Exercise Psychology,* 4(1), pp. 25–49. http://dx.doi.org/10.1080/17 50984X.2010.548528

Biddle, S. J. H., Coalter, F., O'Donovan, T., MacBeth, J., Nevill, M. and Whitehead, S., 2004. *Increasing demand for sport and physical activity by girls.* Edinburgh: Sport Scotland.

Biddle, S. J. H., Cury, F., Goudas, M., Sarrazin, P., Famose, J. P. and Durand, M., 1995. Development of scales to measure perceived physical education class climate: A cross-national project. *British Journal of Educational Psychology,* 65(3), pp. 341–558.

Biddle, S. J. H., Wang, C. K. J., Kavussanu, M. and Spray, C. M., 2003. Correlates of achievement goal orientations in physical activity: A systematic review of research. *European Journal of Sport Science,* 3(5), pp. 1–20.

Biddle, S. J. H., Whitehead, S. H., O'Donovan, T. M. and Nevill, M. E., 2005. Correlates of participation in physical activity of adolescent girls: A systematic review of recent literature. *Journal of Physical Activity and Health,* 2(4), pp. 423–434.

Birchwood, D., Roberts, K. and Pollock, G., 2008. Explaining differences in sport participation rates among young adults: Evidence from the South Caucasus. *European Physical Education Review,* 14(3), pp. 283–298.

Bourdieu, P., 1984. *Distinction: A social critique of the judgement of taste.* Cambridge, MA: Harvard University Press.

Brudzynski, L. and Ebben, W. P., 2010. Body image as a motivator and barrier to exercise participation. *International Journal of Exercise Science,* 3(1), pp. 14–24.

Brustad, R. J., 1992. Integrating socialization influences into the study of children's motivation in sport. *Journal of Sport & Exercise Psychology,* 14(1), pp. 59–77.

Brustad, R. J., 1993. Who will go out and play? Parental and psychological influences on children's attraction to physical activity. *Pediatric Exercise Science,* 5(3), pp. 210–223.

Bungum, T., Dowda, M., Weston, A., Trost, S. G. and Pate, R. R., 2000. Correlates of physical activity in male and female youth. *Pediatric Exercise Science*, 12(1), pp. 71–79.

Burch, W., 1969. Social circles of leisure: Competing explanations. *Journal of Leisure Research*, 41(3), pp. 125–147.

Carson, V., 2016. Cross-sectional and longitudinal associations between parental support and children's physical activity in the early years. *Journal of Physical Activity and Health*, 13(6), pp. 611–616.

Casper, J. M., Bocarro, J. N., Kanters, M. A. and Floyd, M. F., 2011. 'Just let me play!'–understanding constraints that limit adolescent sport participation. *Journal of Physical Activity and Health*, 8(Supplement 1), pp. S32–S39.

Coakley, J. and White, A., 1992. Making decisions: Gender and sport participation among British adolescents. *Sociology of Sport Journal*, 9(1), pp. 20–35.

Coleman, L., Cox, L. and Roker, D., 2008. Girls and young women's participation in physical activity: Psychological and social influences. *Health Education Research*, 23(4), pp. 633–647. http://dx.doi.org/10.1093/her/cym040

Côté, J., Horton, S., MacDonald, D. and Wilkes, S., 2009. The benefits of sampling sports during childhood. *Physical and Health Education Journal*, 74(4), pp. 6–11.

Cox, L., Coleman, L. and Roker, D., 2006. *Understanding participation in sport: What determines sports participation among 15–19 year old women?* Research Conducted by: Trust for the Study of Adolescence. London: Sport England.

Dagkas, S. and Stathi, A., 2007. Exploring social and environmental factors affecting adolescents' participation in physical activity. *European Physical Education Review*, 13(3), pp. 369–384.

Deci, E. L. and Ryan, R. M., 1985. *Intrinsic motivation and self-determination in human behavior*. New York: Plenum Publishing.

Dovey, S. M., Reeder, A. I. and Chalmers, D. J., 1998. Continuity and change in sporting and leisure time physical activities during adolescence. *British Journal of Sports Medicine*, 32(1), pp. 53–57. http://dx.doi.org/10.1136/bjsm.32.1.53

Duncan, J. M., Al-Nakeeb, Y., Nevill, A. and Jones, M. V., 2004. Body image and physical activity in British secondary school children. *European Physical Education Review*, 10(3), pp. 243–260.

Duncan, M., Woodfield, L., Al-Nakeeb, Y. and Nevill, A., 2002. The impact of socio-economic status on the physical activity levels of British secondary school children. *European Journal of Physical Education*, 7(1), pp. 30–44.

Eccles, J., Barber, B. L., Stone, M. and Hunt, J., 2003. Extracurricular activities and adolescent development. *Journal of Social Issues*, 59(4), pp. 865–889.

Edwardson, C. L. and Gorely, T., 2010. Parental influences on different types and intensities of physical activity in youth: A systematic review. *Psychology of Sport and Exercise*, 11(6), pp. 522–535.

Eurostat, 2014. *Sport and physical activity report*. Special Eurobarometer 412. Brussels: European Commission.

Flintoff, A. and Scraton, S., 2001. Stepping into active leisure? Young women's perceptions of active lifestyles and their experiences of school physical education. *Sport, Education and Society*, 6(1), pp. 5–21.

Fox, K., 2000. Review of evidence on the impact of exercise on self esteem. In: S. Biddle, K. Fox, and S. Boutcher, eds. *Physical activity and psychological well-being*. London: Routledge, pp. 88–117.

Fraser-Thomas, J. and Côté, J., 2009. Understanding adolescents' positive and negative developmental experiences in sport. *The Sport Psychologist*, 23, pp. 3–23.

Fraser-Thomas, J., Côté, J. and Deakin, J., 2005. Youth sport programs: An avenue to foster positive youth development. *Physical Education and Sport Pedagogy*, 10(1), pp. 19–40.

Garcia, A. W. and King, A. C., 1991. Predicting long term adherence to aerobic exercise: A comparison of two models. *Journal of Sport and Exercise Psychology*, 13(4), pp. 394–410.

Gershuny, J., 2003. *Time, through the lifecourse, in the family*. ISER Working Paper 2003–3. Colchester: University of Essex.

Godbey, G. C., 2005. Time as a constraint to leisure. In: E. L. Jackson, ed. *Constraints to leisure*. State College, PA: Venture Publishing, pp. 185–200.

Godin, G. and Shephard, R. J., 1986. Psychological factors influencing intentions to exercise of young students from grades 7 to 9. *Research Quarterly for Exercise and Sport*, 57(1), pp. 41–52.

Goretzki, J. and Esser, A., 2008. *Project 'experience of sport' research debrief* [online]. London: Henley Centre HeadlightVision. Available at https://www.sport-england.org/media/3707/quality_of_sporting_experience.pdf

Grant, B. C., 2001. 'You're never too old': Beliefs about physical activity and playing sport in later life. *Ageing and Society*, 21(6), pp. 777–798.

Greenwood-Parr, M. and Oslin, J., 1998. Promoting lifelong involvement through physical activity. *Journal of Physical Education, Recreation and Dance*, 69(2), pp. 72–76.

Hagger, M. S., Chatzisarantis, N. and Biddle, S.J.H., 2001. The influence of self-efficacy and past behaviour on the physical activity intentions of young people. *Journal of Sports Sciences*, 19, pp. 711–725.

Hills, L., 2007. Friendship, physicality, and physical education: An exploration of the social and embodied dynamics of girls' physical education experiences. *Sport, Education and Society*, 12(3), pp. 317–336.

Holt, N. L. and Jones, M. I., 2008. Future directions for positive youth development and sport. In: N. L. Holt, ed. *Positive youth development through sport*. London: Routledge, pp. 122–132.

Horn, D. B., O'Neill, J. R., Pfeiffer, K. A., Dowda, M. and Pate, R. R., 2008. Predictors of physical activity in the transition after high school among young women. *Journal of Physical Activity and Health*, 5(2), pp. 275–285.

Hume, C., Salmon, J. and Ball, K., 2005. Children's perceptions of their home and neighbourhood environments, and their association with objectively measured physical activity: a qualitative and quantitative study. *Health Education Research*, 20(1), pp. 1–13.

Khan, H., 2013. *5 Hours a day: Systemic innovation for an ageing population*. NESTA. Available at: <www.nesta.org.uk/sites/default/files/five_hours_a_day_jan13.pdf>.

Kirk, D., 2004. Sport and early learning experiences. In: N. Rowe, ed. *Driving up participation: The challenge for sport*. London: Sport England, pp. 67–76.

Kirk, D., 2005. Physical education, youth sport and lifelong participation: The importance of early learning experiences. *European Physical Education Review*, 11(3), pp. 239–255.

Kirkwood, T., 2006. Ageing: Too fast by mistake. *Nature*, 444(7122), pp. 1015–1016.

Kyle, G., Absher, J., Norman, W., Hammitt, W. and Jodice, L., 2007. A modified involvement scale. *Leisure Studies*, 26(4), pp. 399–427. http://dx.doi.org/10.1080/02614360600896668

Kyle, G. and Chick, G., 2004. Enduring leisure involvement: The importance of personal relationships. *Leisure Studies*, 23(3), pp. 243–266.

Lewko, J. H. and Greendorfer, S. L., 1978. Family influences and sex differences in children's socialization into sport: A review. In: D. M. Landers and R. W. Christina, eds. *Psychology of motor behaviour and sport*. Champaign, IL: Human Kinetics, pp. 287–300.

Long, J., 2004. Sport and the ageing population: Do older people have a place in driving up participation in sport? In: N. Rowe, ed. *Driving up participation: The challenge for sport*. London: Sport England. pp. 26–36.

Luke, M. D. and Sinclair, G.D., 1991. Gender differences in adolescents' attitudes towards school physical education. *Journal of Teaching in Physical Education*, 11, pp. 31–46.

Lundvall, S., 2015. Physical literacy in the field of physical education: A challenge and a possibility. *Journal of Sport and Health Science*, 4(2), pp. 113–118.

Malina, R. M., 1996. Tracking of physical activity and physical fitness across the lifespan. *Research Quarterly for Exercise and Sport*, 67(3 Supplement), pp. 48–57.

Matthews, P., Xu, D., Matusiak, M. and Prior, G., 2016. *Taking part: Findings from the longitudinal survey waves 1 to 3*. TNS BMRB. London: Department for Culture Media and Sport.

McMurray, R. G., Bradley, C. B., Harrell, J. S., Bernthal, P. R., Frauman, A. C. and Bangdiwala, S. I., 1993. Parental influences on childhood fitness and activity patterns. *Research Quarterly for Exercise and Sport*, 64(3), pp. 249–255.

McPherson, B. D. and Brown, B. A., 1988. The structure, processes, and consequences of sport for children. In: F. L. Smoll, R. A. Magill, and M. J. Ash, eds. *Children in sport*. 3rd ed. Champaign, IL: Human Kinetics, pp. 265–286.

MORI, 2003. *Young people and sport in England: 2002*. London: Sport England.

Mulvihill, C., Rivers, K. and Aggleton, P., 2000. Views of young people towards physical activity: Determinants and barriers to involvement. *Health Education*, 100(5), pp. 190–199. http://dx.doi.org/10.1108/09654280010343555

Newman, B. and Newman, P., 1995. *Development through life: A psychosocial approach*. New York: Brooks/Cole Publishing Co.

Ntoumanis, N., 2001. A self determination approach to the understanding of motivation in physical education. *British Journal of Educational Psychology*, 71(2), pp. 225–242.

Ntoumanis, N., 2002. Motivational clusters in a sample of British physical education classes. *Psychology of Sport and Exercise*, 3(3), pp. 177–194.

Office for National Statistics, 2013. *What does the 2011 Census tell us about older people*. Available at: <www.ons.gov.uk/peoplepopulationandcommunity/birthsdeathsandmarriages/ageing>.

Pelletier, L. G., Fortier, M. S., Vallerand, R. J., Tuson, K. M., Briere, N. M. and Blais, M. R., 1995. Toward a new measure of intrinsic motivation, extrinsic motivation, and amotivation in sports: The sports motivation scale (SMS). *Journal of Sport and Exercise Psychology*, 17(1), pp. 35–53.

Roberts, K. and Brodie, D., 1992. *Inner city sport: Who plays, and what are the benefits?* Culemborg, The Netherlands: Giordano Bruno.

Roberts, K., Minten, J., Chadwick, C., Lamb, K. and Brodie, D., 1991. Sporting lives: A case study of leisure careers. *Society and Leisure*, 14(1), pp. 261–284.

Rowe, N. F., 2012. An examination of the importance and satisfaction sports participants attach to volunteering support contextualized within a broader measure of satisfaction with the quality of the sporting experience. *International Journal of Sport Policy and Politics*, 4(2), pp. 159–172. http://dx.doi.org/10.1080/19406 940.2012.656680

Rowe, N. F., Adams, R. and Beasley, N., 2004. Driving up participation in sport: The social context, the trends, the prospects and the challenges. In: N. Rowe, ed. *Driving up participation: The challenge for sport*. London: Sport England, pp. 6–13.

Rowe, N. F. and Radford, J., Unpublished 2010. *The social physics of sport- static, turbulence and volatility – and why these things matter*. Sport England Internal Research Seminar Series.

Sallis, J. F., Conway, T. L., Prochaska, J. J., McKenzie, T. L., Marshall, S. J. and Brown, M., 2001. The association of school environments with youth physical activity. *American Journal of Public Health*, 91(4), pp. 618–620.

Sallis, J. F. and McKenzie, T. L., 1991. Physical education's role in public health. *Research Quarterly for Exercise and Sport*, 62(2), pp. 124–137.

Sallis, J. F., Prochaska, J. J., Taylor, W. C., Hill, J. O. and Geraci, J. C., 1999. Correlates of physical activity in a national sample of girls and boys in grades 4 through 12. *Health Psychology*, 18(4), pp. 410–415.

Scheerder, J., Thomis, M., Vanreusel, B., Lefevre, J., Renson, R., Enynde, B. V. and Beunen, G. P., 2005. Sports participation among females from adolescence to adulthood: A longitudinal study. *International Review for the Sociology of Sport*, 41(3), pp. 413–430.

Schutzer, K. A. and Graves, B. S., 2004. Barriers and motivations to exercise in older adults. *Preventive Medicine*, 39(5), pp. 1056–1061.

Scott, D. and Godbey, G. G., 1992. An analysis of adult play groups: Social versus serious participation in contract bridge. *Leisure Sciences*, 14(1), pp. 47–67.

Shephard, R. J. and Trudeau, F., 2000. The legacy of physical education: Influences on adult lifestyle. *Pediatric Exercise Science*, 12(1), pp. 34–50.

Slater, A., 2011. Gender differences in adolescent sport participation, teasing, self-objectification and body image concerns. *Journal of Adolescence*, 34(3), pp. 455–463.

Smith, A. L., 1999. Perceptions of peer relationships and physical activity participation in early adolescence. *Journal of Sport and Exercise Psychology*, 21(4), pp. 329–350.

Stodden, D. F., Goodway, J. D., Langendorfer, S. J., Roberton, M. A., Rudisill, M. E., Garcia, C. and Garcia, L. E., 2008. A developmental perspective on the role of motor skill competence in physical activity: An emergent relationship. *Quest*, 60(2), pp. 290–306. http://dx.doi.org/10.1080/00336297.2008.10483582

Stuij, M., 2015. Habitus and social class: A case study on socialisation into sports and exercise. *Sport, Education and Society*, 20(6), pp. 780–798. http://dx.doi.org/ 10.1080/13573322.2013.827568

Tammelin, T., Näyhä, S., Hills, A. P. and Järvelin, M. R., 2003. Adolescent participation in sports and adult physical activity. *American Journal of Preventive Medicine*, 24(1), pp. 22–28.

Taylor, I. M., Ntounamis, N., Standage, M. and Spray, C. M., 2010. Motivational predictors of physical education students' effort, exercise intentions and leisure-time physical activity: A multilevel linear growth analysis. *Journal of Sport & Exercise Psychology*, 32(1), pp. 99–120.

Telama, R., 1998. Psychological background of a physically active lifestyle among European youth. In: R. Naul, K. Hardman, M. Pieron, and B. Skirsted, eds. *Physical activity and active lifestyles of children and youth*. Schorndorf: Karl Hofmann, pp. 63–74.

Telama, R., Yang, X., Hirvensalo, M. and Raitakari, O., 2006. Participation in organised youth sport as a predictor of adult physical activity: A 21 year longitudinal study. *Pediatric Exercise Science*, 17, pp. 76–88.

Telama, R., Yang, X., Laakso, L. and Viikari, J., 1997. Physical activity in childhood and adolescence as predictor of physical activity in young adulthood. *American Journal of Preventive Medicine*, 13(4), pp. 317–323.

Ulrich, B. D., 1987. Perceptions of physical competence, motor competence, and participation in organized sport: Their interrelationships in young children. *Research Quarterly for Exercise and Sport*, 58(1), pp. 57–67.

Van Bottenburg, M., Rijnen, B. and van Sterkenburg, J., 2005. *Sports participation in the European Union: Trends and differences*. Nieuwegein, Netherlands: Arko Sports Media.

Vanreusel, B., Renson, R., Beunen, G., Claessens, A. L., Lefevre, J., Lysens, R. and Eynde, B. V., 1997. A longitudinal study of youth sport participation and adherence to sport in adulthood. *International Review for the Sociology of Sport*, 32(4), pp. 373–387.

Van Tuyckom, C., Scheerder, J. and Bracke, P., 2010. Gender and age inequalities in regular sports participation: A cross-national study of 25 European countries. *Journal of Sports Sciences*, 28(10), pp. 1077–1084. http://dx.doi.org/10.1080/02640414.2010.492229

Viira, R. and Raudsepp, L., 2000. Achievement goal orientations, beliefs about sport success and sport emotions as related to moderate to vigorous physical activity of adolescents. *Psychology and Health*, 15(5), pp. 625–633.

Wankel, L. M., 1993. The importance of enjoyment to adherence and psychological benefits from physical activity. *International Journal of Sport Psychology*, 24(2), pp. 151–169.

Wankel, L. M. and Kreisel, P. S. J., 1985. Factors underlying enjoyment of youth sports: Sport and age group comparisons. *Journal of Sport Psychology*, 7(1), pp. 51–64.

Wearing, B., 1995. Leisure and resistance in an ageing society. *Leisure Studies*, 14(4), pp. 263–279.

Weiss, M. R., 1987. Self esteem and achievement in children's sport and physical activity. In: D. Gould and M. R. Weiss, eds. *Advances in pediatric sport sciences, vol. 2: Behavioural issues*. Champaign, IL: Human Kinetics, pp. 87–119.

Weiss, M. R., 2013. Back to the future: Research trends in youth motivation and physical activity. *Pediatric Exercise Science*, 25(4), pp. 561–572.

Weiss, M. R. and Smith, A. L., 2002. Friendship quality in youth sport: Relationship to age, gender and motivational variables. *Journal of Sport and Exercise Psychology*, 24(4), pp. 420–437.

Whitehead, M. ed., 2010. *Physical literacy throughout the lifecourse*. London: Routledge.

Wickstrom, R., 1983. *Fundamental motor patterns*. 3rd ed. Philadelphia: Lea & Febiger.

Widdop, P., Cutts, D. and Jarvie, G., 2016. Omnivorousness in sport: The importance of social capital and networks. *International Review for the Sociology of Sport*, 51(5), pp. 596–616.

Wilkinson, S., Littlefair, D. and Barlow-Meade, L., 2013. What is recognised as ability in physical education? A systematic appraisal of how ability and ability differences are socially constructed within mainstream secondary school physical education. *European Physical Education Review*, 19(2), pp. 147–164.

Williamson, D. F., Kahn, H. S., Remington, P. L. and Anda, R. F., 1990. The 10-year incidence of overweight and major weight gain in U.S. adults. *Archives of Internal Medicine*, 150(3), pp. 665–672.

Wold, B. and Anderssen, N., 1992. Health promotion aspects of family and peer influences on sport participation. *International Journal of Sport Psychology*, 23(4), pp. 343–359.

Women's Sport and Fitness Foundation, 2012. *Changing the game for girls*. Available at: <http://wsff.org.uk/sites/wsff.org.uk/files/Changing_The_Game_For_Girls_Final_0.pdf>.

Wood, L. and Danylchuk, K., 2011. Playing our way: Contributions of social groups to women's continued participation in golf. *Leisure Sciences*, 33(5), pp. 366–381.

Wrotniak, B. H., Epstein, L. H., Dorn, J. M., Jones, K. E. and Kondilis, V. A., 2006. The relationship between motor proficiency and physical activity in children. *Pediatrics*, 118(6), pp. e1758–e1765.

Yang, X., Telama, R. and Laakso, L., 1996. Parents' physical activity, socio-economic status and education as predictors of physical activity and sport among children and youth: A 12 year follow up study. *International Review for the Sociology of Sport*, 31(3), pp. 273–291.

Chapter 6

Sporting capital in England

From measurement process to painting the landscape

Measuring sporting capital – the Sporting Capital Index

In previous chapters I have discussed the public policy challenge facing sport, particularly, but not exclusively in England. I have introduced the theory of sporting capital and explained its potential to support a paradigm shift in public policy intervention; explored other theories of behaviour change that have relevance to physical activity and sporting behaviour, highlighting their strengths and limitations when applied to sports development policy and practice; and I have reviewed the evidence base that links to and tests or supports the core propositions underpinning sporting capital theory. My emphasis now shifts towards new empirical research that seeks for the first time to measure and operationalise sporting capital within the English adult population.

Sporting capital is defined as, "*the stock of physiological, sociological and psychological attributes and competencies that support and motivate an individual to participate in sport and to sustain that participation over time.*" I have made the point earlier that everyone has a certain level of sporting capital just as they have a level of human capital or cultural capital. However, to define how much 'stock' any one individual has of these capitals is not straightforward. Perhaps of all the three 'capitals', human capital is the easiest to measure as it is reflected in the formal qualifications that an individual holds and their years of education. But even here it poses challenges of definition and measurement when human capital also includes the less tangible skills and knowledge that come from years of work experience gained in different kinds of environments, both professional and voluntary, and the interpersonal and leadership skills that are not reflected in formal qualifications. The challenge to quantify sporting capital is even greater, as formal qualifications in, for example, sports studies or coaching although relevant only touch on a relatively small minority of people and do not reflect in a holistic sense the full gamut of attributes that make up sporting capital in its entirety.

I have mentioned earlier in this book that people have an innate sense of both their own level of sporting capital and that of other individuals that they know reasonably well. They of course do not call it 'sporting capital' or even necessarily think of it in these terms. Often it is characterised in terminology such as 'level of sportiness' or people seeing themselves or others as 'a sporty type of person' or 'being good at sport' or having 'good hand eye coordination skills'. However, having an innate sense of sporting capital in oneself and in others is not a sufficiently accurate basis to provide a reliable empirical measure that can be used to test the theory and to inform policy and practice. Something more sophisticated is required than relying solely on a simple measure of 'how do you rate your level of sportiness on a scale of 1 to 10'.

The more sophisticated measure used here is what I refer to as the Sporting Capital Index (SCI). It is a composite measure of an individual's sporting capital on a straightforward scale of 1 to 10 with 1 being low and 10 being high. Reflecting its theoretical foundations, the SCI is constructed from answers to question items across the three domains, physiological, psychological and social[1] (see also Nordern, 2013). The data source used to construct the 'Sporting Capital Index' and to measure and analyse sporting capital levels in England is the Active People Survey (APS). The APS is the largest sport and recreational physical activity survey in Europe. It measures levels of participation in sport and recreational physical activity in the English adult (16 plus) population. The survey, commissioned by Sport England and carried out initially by Ipsos MORI and then by TNS-BMRB, ran continuously, with a one year break in 2006–07, from October 2005 to October 2016 (APS10). The main survey is a stratified random sample design administered by telephone with sample sizes ranging from 364,000 in 2005–06 to 163,000 in the most recent reported year to September 2016 (see Rowe, 2009; Sport England, 2016). The sporting capital survey questions were included in the October 2011 to October 2012 household interview wave of the survey (a sub-sample of the larger telephone administered survey) and consisted of 4,527 interviews[2 3]. The sample was selected on a random probability basis and the results were weighted to be representative of the adult (16 plus) English population. Sport England has now replaced the Active People Survey with the 'Active Lives Survey' which includes young people aged 14 years and over and reports on a wider range of physical activities (Sport England, 2017).

There are many different ways that sporting capital could be measured. The questions included in APS[4] (see also Figure 6.1 for details of the questionnaire content) were designed to provide one way of establishing reliable 'markers' of people's position in relation to each of the three domains and in combination an index of their overall level of sporting capital. The question design drew from existing validated psychometric scales and, in particular, the Physical Self-Perception Profile Manual developed by Fox

---

Physiological domain

During the past 4 weeks, to what extent has your physical health interfered with your normal social activities with family, friends, neighbours or groups?

During the last 4 weeks how much did physical pain interfere with your normal work (including both work outside the home and housework)?

I would like to ask you about your abilities and skills and how you would rate yourself compared with people of your own age and gender (General sporting ability and skills; Mobility/flexibility; Strength; Stamina; Running speed; Agility/balance; Hand eye co-ordination).

Psychological domain

I am going to read out a number of statements and for each one, I would like you to tell me to what extent it is true for you. (I am a sporty person; I would feel a real loss if I was forced to give up playing sport or from ever taking part in sport in the future; I feel completely confident and at ease in situations where people take part in sport or exercise activity; I would be confident about the appearance of my body when taking part in sport or exercise activity).

I would now like to ask you about how confident you are that you would still take part in sport when other things get in the way. How confident are you that you would still take part in sport when…. You are under a lot of stress; You feel you don't have the time; You have to take part alone or without your regular playing companions; Your partner does not want you to take part; It's cold, raining or snowing.

Social domain

To what extent do you agree with the following ……..? Most of my family members regularly take part in sport; Most of my friends regularly take part in sport; Many of the people I work most closely with regularly take part in sport; While at secondary school I regularly took part in organised sport outside of school lessons.

Figure 6.1 Questionnaire constructs used to measure sporting capital

and Corbin (1989) and the Self-Efficacy for Exercise (SEE) scale developed initially by Resnick and Jenkins (2000). The questions relevant to sporting capital followed a raft of detailed questions on sport and recreation participation behaviours that made up the larger APS survey instrument. The question on 'physical abilities and skills' is a measure of perceived ability rather than the ideal of actual objective measured abilities which was not feasible to measure at the time. Inevitably there is some overlap between this measure and those included in the psychological domain and this is an acknowledged weakness that future research should address. Notwithstanding, the review carried out in Chapter 5 showed how important perceived ability is as a motivational factor to take part in sport and physical activity and to this extent it is a strong measure to include in the construction of the overall Sporting Capital Index.

The modelling underpinning the creation of the SCI is complex and details can be found in a Technical Report (Nordern, 2013). Put simply, it seeks to optimise the combined power of the measures in the form of a 10-point index (1 low and 10 high) to explain variations in the probability of an individual participating in sport at threshold levels of at least once a week for 30 minutes' moderate intensity consistent with the definition of sport participation used by Sport England at the time. This is a definition that excludes most forms of walking but includes for example cycling for sport and recreational purposes. The Sporting Capital Index scores are estimated through a three-staged approach to the modelling which initially, using a combination of Factor Analysis and Linear Regression, calculates weights for each individual question. Using further modelling techniques, these 'question weights' are translated into weights for each of the three domains. The process for calculating the weights to apply to the domains is identical to that of applying weights to the questions for each domain. The final domain weights are as follows: physiological domain 0.35; psychological domain 0.36; and the social domain 0.29. Finally, a binary Logistic Regression model was employed to test the relationship between the sporting capital scores and sports participation which through the calculation of 'odds ratios' could be translated into estimates of the probability of participating in sport with changes in individual levels of sporting capital.

Before presenting the results, it is worth emphasising again that there is nothing absolutely definitive in the Sporting Capital Index (SCI) as presented here. The SCI is but one of potentially many ways to empirically test and explore some of the propositions that would be consistent with the theory of sporting capital as outlined in Chapter 3. However, I am confident that the measure, if not perfect, is fit for the purpose in so far as the results are consistent with what we would expect, particularly in the relationship between levels of sporting capital and changes in the probability of participating in sport and in the variations in sporting capital scores across different sub-groups in the population. Although at a very fine grain there may be blurred edges as to whether someone classified on the margins of say an SCI score of 3 might if measured in a different way be classified as a 2 or a 4, the probability of that person being classified as say a 5 or a 1 if measured differently is, I would contend, likely to be very small indeed.

The results that follow provide a fascinating first glimpse into the distribution of sporting capital in England, what I have termed the 'sporting capital landscape'. They show how sporting capital impacts on the probability of participating in sport, how the distribution of sporting capital is socially structured by age, gender and social class and how levels of sporting capital impact on the types of sports in which people take part and those that are likely to be attractive to them. The results show the extent of the challenge for sports development presented through a new lens, not one of negative constraints or misplaced 'opportunities' but one of frustrated potential and capacity for growth. Although the results are limited to experience in England, there are lessons and insights for other countries in the UK, for near neighbours in Europe and for countries further afield such as Australia, New Zealand and Canada which have similar community sports systems facing similar societal challenges associated with stagnating participation rates in sport, structural inequalities, increasing inactivity, poor health and strains on the fabric of social and community cohesion.

How much more likely are people to participate in sport with increases in their levels of sporting capital?

The evidence from the Active People Survey provides empirical support for the relationship between levels of sporting capital and rates of participation in sport. The higher the level of sporting capital, the higher the probability that someone will participate regularly in sport (at least once a week for 30 minutes' moderate intensity) and the lower the level the higher the probability of sedentary behaviours (i.e. of not participating). This is not a straight-line relationship; in fact the relative odds of participating are on average 2.3 times higher with each increase of one SCI point in the sporting capital score. Figure 6.2 shows these changes in the probability of participating in sport with changes in the Sporting Capital Index score.

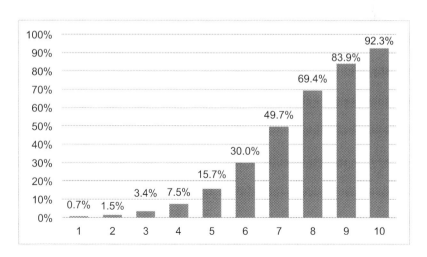

Figure 6.2 Probability of participating in sport (at least once a week moderate intensity) with changes in the Sporting Capital Index Score (1 is low and 10 is high) in the English adult (16 plus) population

Importantly it demonstrates how the relationship between levels of sporting capital and rates of participation is not a linear one. As the SCI scores increase, the probability of participating increases more steeply. The largest increases in rates of participation are seen in the changes between an SCI score of 5 and 6 where the probability of participating increases from 15.7 percent to 30 percent and between a SCI score of 6 and 7 where the probability increases from 30 percent to 50 percent. It is between a sporting capital score of 7 and 8 that the probability of participating regularly in sport exceeds the probability of not participating (i.e. is greater than 50 percent).

Further analysis shows that there are subtle differences in the relationship between participation and sporting capital with age. Figure 6.3 shows how the probability of participating at different levels of sporting capital changes with age. Although the general shape of the relationship is similar for all age groups, the younger age groups have a higher probability of participating at any given level of sporting capital than their older counterparts. This is particularly the case in the mid range levels of sporting capital (SCI scores of 5 to 8). *These results suggest that as people get older the relative impact of barriers to participating get higher and hence require*

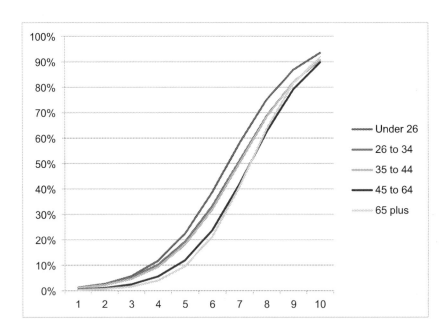

Figure 6.3 Probability of participating in sport (at least once a week moderate intensity) with changes in the Sporting Capital Index score by age (1 is low and 10 is high) in the English adult (16 plus) population

a higher level of sporting capital to overcome them. The good news is that the returns in terms of increased probabilities of participation are greater for smaller increases in sporting capital amongst the young than they are for the older age groups.

The above analysis provides empirical support for the central theoretical proposition underpinning sporting capital theory of a relationship between regular participation in sport and levels of sporting capital. As important as this relationship is to public policy, it is also the nature of the relationship in terms of the 'shape of the curve' that has significant implications for those designing and delivering public programmes and projects. Firstly and importantly, it suggests that *if those intervening can demonstrate that they have increased levels of sporting capital amongst their targeted participants, they can say with confidence that they have also increased the number of regular sports participants.* Secondly and more specifically, the results show that *the largest potential gains for public policy is to shift those with sporting capital levels of 5 and 6 to levels of 7 and 8.* Beyond this, the theory would suggest that there is more to be gained from these shifts than a short-term increase in participation. For example a move from a sporting capital level of 5 to one of 8 would result in both immediate short-term increases in participation *and* the prospects of longer term sustained behaviour change as individuals' capacity and motivation to participate increases and they become more resilient to external barriers and obstacles faced over their life-course. Further, the theory would suggest the possibility of a positive feedback loop being created with increased participation building further sporting capital and increased sporting capital in turn increasing participation. The results also suggest that young people's participation is more sensitive to changes in sporting capital than older people and that increases in sporting capital amongst the young will deliver bigger immediate increases in participation than the equivalent increase would for older age groups.

Are we a sporting nation – what are the levels of sporting capital in England?

The stock of sporting capital, unlike the direct experience of participation, or for that matter, levels of fitness, can be built up and stored over time. However, sporting capital doesn't necessarily last forever. The theory suggests that this stock does have a shelf life and without use (participation) that it will depreciate over time with the speed, or rate of depreciation varying from individual to individual. However, as discussed earlier in this book, unlike participation which is transient in nature and subject to short-term fluctuations of dropping in, dropping out, a week off here, a month off there, sporting capital is more durable. Sporting capital may be thought of as the 'locked in potential for participation' and to this extent is a better underlying measure of the 'sportiness' of an individual, local community, region or nation than participation rates per se. The expression or realisation of that locked in potential in terms of actual participation is, however, mediated by the external constraints and barriers that impact on an individual, including other competing demands for their time, the accessibility and quality of opportunities available and the price at which they can be accessed (see Chapters 3 and 5).

As we have seen earlier, sporting capital has relevance at a range of geographical levels from the individual household to neighbourhoods and communities and up to the level of the nation and international comparisons. Much has been reported on the rates of participation and numbers of sport participants in England (and other countries), but prior to this research the aggregate level of sporting capital in a nation has never been explored or measured. This research shows that the mean Sporting Capital Index score (on a scale of 1 to 10) for the adult population aged 16 and over in England is 5.7. Figure 6.4 shows how the level of sporting capital in England is distributed across the 10-point SCI scale. Although the distribution takes the general form of a 'normal distribution', it is slightly skewed towards the positive end of the scale. So for example there are more people with a Sporting Capital Index score of 9 than a score of 2 and more with a score of 8 than of 3.

Judgement on how 'sporty' a country is must be a relative one. However, I would contend that at least from a community sport perspective, as

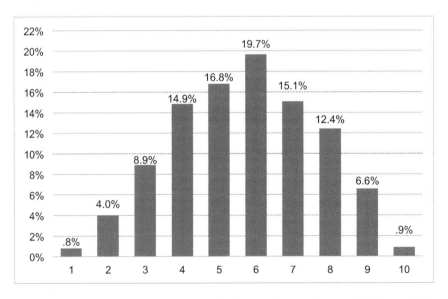

Figure 6.4 Distribution of sporting capital (1 is low and 10 is high) in the English adult (16 plus) population

opposed to an elite sport one, the judgement of a nation's sportiness is best assessed by measurement of sporting capital in the population at any given time rather than levels of participation, although the two as we have seen are closely related. Given the lack of comparative data with other countries, it is not possible to say whether or not the levels of sporting capital shown in Figure 6.4 would classify England as a highly ranked 'sporting nation'. There is no doubt that England does have a rich history and tradition of sport, factors that culturally would dispose it towards relatively high levels of sporting capital compared with many other countries in the world. However, although the evidence on sporting capital is not available, it would be reasonable to assume that countries like Sweden, Norway, Denmark and Finland that have higher rates of participation in sport than we find in England also have higher levels of sporting capital, both in aggregate and in the distribution across different socio-demographic groups. The alternative is that they have fewer external constraints and barriers that make participation more difficult. The reality is almost certainly a combination of these two factors. It would be interesting to obtain empirical evidence to explore this further.

The distribution of sporting capital by age, gender and social class

As we have seen earlier in Chapter 2, the levels of participation in sport in England are structured socially and economically with men historically participating at higher rates than women, the young participating more than the old and those in the higher social class groups having higher rates of participation than those in the lower groups. Given the strong relationship between participation in sport and sporting capital, it is to be expected that Sporting Capital Index scores will vary by age, gender and social class in similar ways. However, as discussed above, sporting capital is not a measure of participation; it is a measure of the antecedents to participation in terms of the attributes/capacities that in combination increase individual motivation and hence the probability of participating in sport and to sustain that participation over time. To this extent it cannot be assumed that the profile of sporting capital across different social groups and associated inequalities will match the profile of participation across those groups.

Figure 6.5 shows how mean levels of sporting capital change with age. It is interesting to note that there is little change in the levels between the ages of 16 and the late 30s and early 40s, and yet we know that participation rates in sport decline significantly over the same ages, by about 40 percent. How can this be the case? These results suggest that while the locked in potential to participate, i.e. the stock of sporting capital, is maintained until the early 40s, the external barriers and constraints that make participation more difficult increase. These barriers include, for example, the pressures

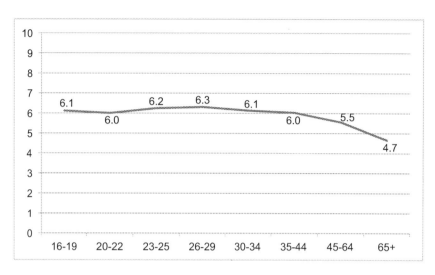

Figure 6.5 Sporting Capital Index mean score by age (1 is low and 10 is high) in the English adult (16 plus) population

of work, the demands of raising a family, other competing demands for time including other leisure choices, a lack of suitable places to play or at least an awareness of the opportunities available and financial pressures that impact on affordability. The outcome is an increasing negative balance sheet between the levels of sporting capital (and hence motivation) on the one hand and the barriers and constraints to participation, on the other hand, leading to drop out and non participation with age. The longer term consequence of this inactivity is a slow but ultimately inevitable attrition in an individual's stock of sporting capital. We see this after the age of 44 years when there is a significant decline in mean sporting capital scores which inevitably is associated with continued declines in participation. Many in this age group will look back to their younger selves and will see their 'sporting capital' as a thing of the past that was enjoyed at the time but is not to be regained or even aspired to now they are older. Yet the theory would suggest that it is never too late to rebuild sporting capital levels, although the longer someone has been away from participating the more difficult this becomes.

We know that participation rates in sport are socially structured and that these differences have proved stubbornly difficult to shift despite nearly 50 years of public policy focus (see Chapter 2). A fundamental question, however, has remained unanswered and it is to what extent these expressions of inequalities in behaviour are underpinned by inequalities in the antecedents to participation in the form of people's psychological, social

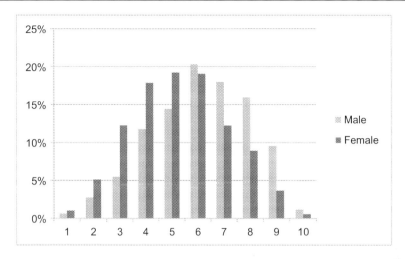

Figure 6.6 Distribution of Sporting Capital Index scores by gender (1 is low and 10 is high) in the English adult (16 plus) population

and physical relationship to sport, i.e. in terms of their levels of sporting capital. Figure 6.6 shows how the distribution of sporting capital scores varies by gender. On average men have a sporting capital level that is almost one point higher than that found for women (6.1 to 5.3). This may not seem to be significant, but as we have seen earlier (in Figure 6.2), the difference in the probability of participating between those on an SCI score of 5 and those on a score of 6 is considerable, from 15.7 percent to 30 percent, respectively. The drop in the population percentages between Sporting Capital Index scores of 6 and 8 is worth highlighting. This drop is much greater for women than it is for men and has significant impacts on the relative probabilities for participating in sport, which is 69 percent for someone with a score of 8 compared with 30 percent for those with an SCI score of 6. Similar patterns are found when we examine the variations in levels of sporting capital by social class[5]. The mean Sporting Capital Index score for those in the upper social class groups (NS-SEC 1–4) is 6.0 compared with a mean score of 5.3 for those in the lower social class groups (NS-SEC 5–8) and again this difference impacts significantly on the probabilities of participating in sport. Figure 6.7 shows the distribution of sporting capital between different social class groups and shows how it is skewed towards the lower end of the scale for those in NS-SEC 5–8 and towards the upper end of the scale for those in NS-SEC 1–4. Interestingly, this pattern is similar to the one for gender and has a similar scale of impact on the probability of participating in sport. So the answer to the question posed earlier is clear, *inequalities in community sport are socially structured both in the*

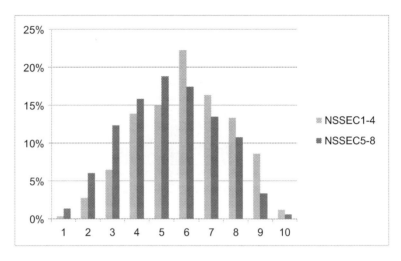

Figure 6.7 Distribution of Sporting Capital Index scores by social class (1 is low and 10 is high) in the English adult (16 plus) population

expressions of behaviour (participation) and in the antecedent capacities that underpin that behaviour (sporting capital).

Summary and implications

In summary, what do these empirical findings tell us so far about the state of sport in England? I would suggest on the positive side that it would not be unreasonable to argue that we may consider England to be a 'sporting nation' with a mean Sporting Capital Index score of 5.7 and over a third of the population (35 percent) with a mean SCI score of 7 and above. However, we should also recognise that nearly three in 10 of the adult population (29 percent) have a Sporting Capital Index score of 4 or less with associated very low probabilities of participating in sport. The probability of participating for people on these low levels of sporting capital range from less than 15 percent (SCI score of 4) to less than 1 percent (SCI score of 1) and the challenges to engage them in sport are extremely high if not in some cases impossible. Perhaps of even greater concern is the empirical evidence that shows that there are significant structural inequalities in the levels of sporting capital related to age, gender and social class. There are important implications for public policy from these findings. These are not inequalities in behaviour but inequalities in the more fundamental things that shape and influence that behaviour. If we are to continue to have public policy aspirations to increase population-wide levels of participation in sport and to reduce inequalities in participation, we must address the fundamental inequalities that drive these differences. There are two ways that this can be done. One is to increase the overall levels of sporting capital in the population and to reduce the social inequalities in how it is distributed. The other is to increase the opportunities available and to decrease the constraints and barriers that prevent people from expressing their sporting preferences in a tangible way. The relative merits of each approach were discussed in Chapter 3 and are picked up again in Chapters 8 and 9.

Notes

1 The 'Creating Sporting Capital Scores – Technical document' was prepared by Oliver Norden at TNS-BMRB who was responsible for the statistical model design and testing. The research was commissioned by StreetGames and overseen by Nick Rowe who was responsible for developing the original conceptual thinking around Sporting Capital. Data was provided by Sport England.
2 The original Sporting Capital Index was created in summer 2012 based on data from the 1st quarter (Q1) of Active People Survey APS6 (October 2011 to January 2012 – 1,429 interviews). Analysis was then conducted on the sporting capital scores for the sample from that quarter. However, the amount of demographic analysis was limited due to the relatively modest sample size of a single quarter. In March/April 2013 the full APS6 dataset could be utilised for both a repeat of the modelling procedure (to check consistency) and to allow more in-depth analysis to be carried out, both in terms of more detailed analysis of sub-group differences and more comprehensive analysis topics.
3 The sporting capital questions were added onto the Active People 6 in-home, face-to-face survey. The survey consisted of a clustered (by Postcode), probability sample design taken from the PAF (Postcode Address File), where only one member of the household was chosen randomly for interview. The data has been weighted to account for differences in selection probabilities as well as non-response differentials, and hence is representative of the English population. The survey ran from October 2011 to October 2012 and consisted of 4,527 interviews once missing data was removed.
4 The questionnaire from which the Sporting Capital Index was derived is as follows:

Sporting Capital Questionnaire

Physiological domain
I would now like to ask you some questions about factors which may or may not affect your participation in activities.

Physical health
During the past 4 weeks, to what extent has your physical health interfered with your normal social activities with family, friends, neighbours or groups?
1. Not at all
2. A little bit
3. Moderately
4. Quite a bit

5. Extremely
6. INTERVIEWER DO NOT READ OUT: Don't know
7. INTERVIEWER DO NOT READ OUT: Refused
[Ask All]
During the last 4 weeks how much did *physical pain* interfere with your normal work (including both work outside the home and housework)?
1. Not at all
2. A little bit
3. Moderately
4. Quite a bit
5. Extremely
6. INTERVIEWER DO NOT READ OUT: Don't know
7. INTERVIEWER DO NOT READ OUT: Refused

Physical competency
[ASK ALL]
I would like to ask you about your abilities and skills and how you would rate yourself compared with people of your own age and gender
So thinking about your . . . .
1. General sporting ability and skills
2. Mobility/flexibility
3. Strength
4. Stamina
5. Running speed
6. Agility/balance
7. Hand eye coordination
(INTERVIEWER ADD IF NECESSARY: How would you rate yourself compared with people of your own age and gender?)
Would you say you are . . .
a) Much better than most
b) A bit better than most
c) About average
d) A bit worse than most
e) Much worse than most
f) INTERVIEWER DO NOT READ OUT: Don't know
g) INTERVIEWER DO NOT READ OUT: Refused

Psychological domain
[ASK ALL]
I am going to read out a number of statements and for each one, I would like you to tell me to what extent it is true for you.
1. I am a sporty person
2. I would feel a real loss if I was forced to give up playing sport or from ever taking part in sport in the future
3. I feel completely confident and at ease in situations where people take part in sport or exercise activity
4. I would be confident about the appearance of my body when taking part in sport or exercise activity
So is this . . . . .

a) Very true for you
b) Somewhat true for you
c) Somewhat untrue for you
d) Not at all true for you
e) INTERVIEWER DO NOT READ OUT: Don't know
f) INTERVIEWER DO NOT READ OUT: Refused
[For those who currently take part in sport]

I would now like to ask you about how confident you are that you would still take part in sport when other things get in the way. On a scale of 1 to 5, where 1 is not at all confident and 5 is completely confident . . . . . .
How confident are you that you would still take part in sport when . . .
1. You are under a lot of stress.
2. You feel you don't have the time
3. You have to take part alone or without your regular playing companions
4. Your partner does not want you to take part
5. It's cold, raining or snowing
   a) Not at all confident
   b) Somewhat confident
   c) Moderately confident
   d) Very confident
   e) Completely confident
   f) INTERVIEWER DO NOT READ OUT: Not applicable
   g) INTERVIEWER DO NOT READ OUT: Don't know
   h) INTERVIEWER DO NOT READ OUT: Refused

Note that those that are filtered around this question because they do not do sport should automatically be placed in 'a) Not at all confident'. If respondents don't have a partner they are coded as 'Not applicable'

Social domain
[ASK ALL]
To what extent do you agree with the following . . . . ?
1. Most of my family members regularly take part in sport
2. Most of my friends regularly take part in sport
3. Many of the people I work most closely with regularly take part in sport
4. While at secondary school I regularly took part in organised sport outside of school lessons

Do you . . .
   a) Completely agree
   b) Somewhat agree
   c) Neither agree or disagree
   d) Somewhat disagree
   e) Completely disagree
   f) INTERVIEWER DO NOT READ OUT: Not applicable
   g) INTERVIEWER DO NOT READ OUT: Don't know
   h) INTERVIEWER DO NOT READ OUT: Refused

If respondents don't work, they are coded as 'Not applicable' to statement 3.

5 Measures of Social Class – the APS uses NS-SEC (National Statistics Socio-economic classification) which is the primary social classification in the United

Kingdom developed by the Office for National Statistics and used across Government. The full version of NS-SEC has 17 main categories. The version intended for most users (the analytic version) has eight categories:

1. Higher managerial and professional occupations
2. Lower managerial and professional occupations
3. Intermediate occupations (clerical, sales, service)
4. Small employers and own account workers
5. Lower supervisory and technical occupations
6. Semi-routine occupations
7. Routine occupations
8. Never worked or long-term unemployed

According to Rose, Devalin and O'Reilly (2005, p. 14) "In terms of its conceptual basis, the NS-SEC follows a well-defined sociological position that employment relations and conditions are central to delineating the structure of socioeconomic positions in modern societies".

"the NS-SEC attempts to make explicit what was latent in SEG categories by reference to employment status characteristics that are widely recognised as significant in the literature (such as mode of payment, promotion prospects and autonomy)."

References

Fox, K. R. and Corbin, C., 1989. The physical self-perception profile: Development and preliminary validation. *Journal of Exercise and Sport Psychology*, 11(4), pp. 408–430.

Nordern, O., 2013. *Creating sporting capital scores: Technical document*. London: BMRB.

Resnick, B. and Jenkins, L., 2000. Testing the reliability and validity of the self-efficacy for exercise scale. *Nursing Research*, 49(3), pp. 154–159.

Rose, R., Devalin, D. and O'Reilly, K., 2005. *The national statistics socio-economic classification: Origins, development and use*. National Statistics. London: Palgrave Macmillan.

Rowe, N. F., 2009. The active people survey: A catalyst for transforming evidence-based sport policy in England. *International Journal of Sport Policy and Politics*, 1(1), pp. 89–98. http://dx.doi.org/10.1080/19406940802681244

Sport England, 2016. Available at: <www.sportengland.org/news-and-features/news/2016/december/8/record-numbers-of-women-getting-active> [accessed 16th May 2017].

Sport England, 2017. *Active lives survey year 1 report*. Available at: <www.sportengland.org/media/11498/active-lives-survey-yr-1-report.pdf> [accessed 16th May 2017].

Chapter 7

Sporting capital in England

A level playing field? Exploring age, gender, social class, and sporting preferences

The previous chapter introduced the Sporting Capital Index as the first ever empirical measure of sporting capital in the English adult population. It provided evidence of the relationship between levels of sporting capital and participation in sport and went on to quantify sporting capital in England showing in aggregate how sporting capital is distributed across the population and the broad structural inequalities in this distribution by age, gender and social class. In this chapter I 'peel back the onion' to reveal another layer of insight and understanding of these structural inequalities by examining in greater depth the building blocks of sporting capital as reflected in individual responses to question items and the physiological, psychological and social domain scores. I then go on to examine the relationship between levels of sporting capital and individual sporting preferences to reveal insights that impact on sports policy generally and the policies and practices of national governing bodies of sport in particular.

Sporting capital – a focus on age and gender

Figure 7.1 shows how mean Sporting Capital Index scores vary by age and gender. We have seen earlier how levels of sporting capital remain broadly unchanged until people reach their late 30s to early 40s, and how this applies to both genders. However, it is the 'gender gap' in levels of sporting capital across all age groups that comes across most clearly and unambiguously. Perhaps the most telling statistic, given the evidence reviewed in Chapter 5 which showed how important younger age experience is on predicting later life involvement in sport, is that this gap is at its largest for the youngest age group. Interestingly, the gap in sporting capital between men and women starts to narrow from the age of 35 years onwards which perhaps coincides with the decline in participation in team sports during these years for many men and the maintenance of women's involvement in more informal fitness related activities in their later years.

It is interesting to first examine how the domain scores vary across different social groups by age and gender. Sporting capital is made up of three

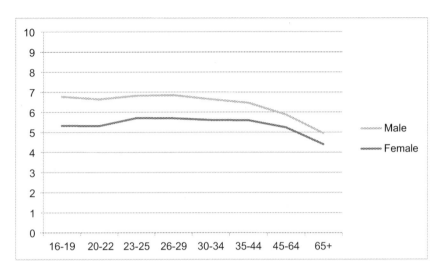

Figure 7.1 Sporting capital mean scores (1 is low and 10 is high) by age and gender in the adult (16 plus) English population

domains, the psychological, social and physiological. In turn these domains are measured by a series of questions that provide markers that are relevant to each domain (see Figure 6.1 in Chapter 6). For example, in the psychological domain questions address factors related to self efficacy in sporting situations, self confidence and identity. In the physiological domain the questions seek to establish markers of people's sporting ability relative to others of the same age and gender in a range of sport-related skills and their overall physical health status. In the social domain there are questions related to social connectedness in sport ranging from how sporty other family members are to the sportiness of friendship networks and work colleagues. As we have seen in the theoretical discussions in Chapters 3 and 4 and in the evidence review in Chapter 5, each domain is important both in its own right and in how it interacts to influence the other domains.

In the English adult population the physiological domain had the highest mean score of 6.5 out of 10 followed by the social domain with a score of 5.9 and the psychological domain with a mean score of 4.5. The low mean score for the psychological domain is an important finding given the relatively high impact this domain has on the overall Sporting Capital Index scores. Figure 7.2 shows the profile of mean domain scores (on a scale of 1 low to 10 high) by age across the adult population in England. As with the overall Sporting Capital Index scores, there is relatively little change with age until people reach their mid 40s. Perhaps unexpectedly, the social domain scores tend to increase with age into the 20s and 30s before declining. The scores

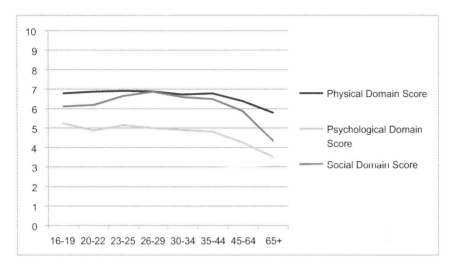

Figure 7.2 Mean domain scores (on a scale of 1 to 10 with 1 low and 10 high) by age in the adult (16 plus) English population

on the psychological domain are considerably and consistently lower than those for the other two domains across all age groups. It is interesting to examine how scores on question items in the psychological domain change with age. Figure 7.3 provides a rating of the scores for a number of question items where the 'net Index score' equals the percentage who agree that it is *'very true for you'* (i.e. a positive response) minus the percentage who agree *'it is not at all true for you'* (a negative response). Apart from 'body confidence' which stays fairly constant between the ages of 16 to 29 years, all the other measures of psychological affect peak in the early 20s and then drop off rapidly after people reach the age of 30 years. By their early 30s those seeing themselves as a *'sporty type of person'* has a negative net rating, i.e. there are more people who agree it is *'not at all true for you'* than agree *'it is completely true for you'*. The net ratings for a sense of real loss *'if I was forced to give up playing sport or from ever taking part in sport in the future'* move into negative territory when people reach their mid 60s.

It is to be expected, given what we know about overall levels of sporting capital and about levels of participation in sport, that the building blocks (domains and question items) of sporting capital would vary in their relative strengths and weaknesses between men and women. Figure 7.4 shows that men score more highly in all three domains than women, but the gap is greatest in the psychological domain where the scores are relatively low for both men and women. Again this is an important finding as it is the psychological domain that has the highest weighting and hence the largest relative

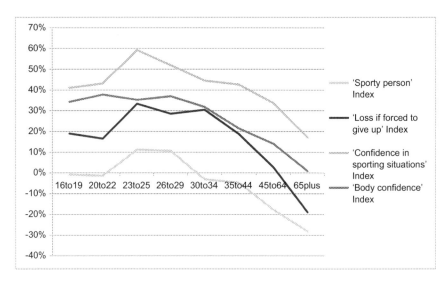

Figure 7.3 Changes in the psychological relationship to sport in the adult (16 plus) English population. Net 'Index Scores' for selected question items in the Psychological domain (the net score is equal to the percent who agree 'it is very true for you' minus the percent who agree it is 'not at all true for you')

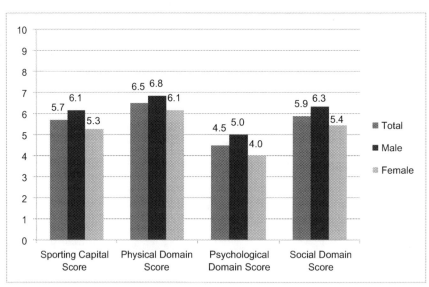

Figure 7.4 Mean domain scores (on a scale of 1 to 10 with 1 low and 10 high) by gender in the adult (16 plus) English population

impact on the overall Sporting Capital Index scores (see Chapter 6). It is worth exploring some of the gender differences in the psychological domain scores in more depth.

A measure in the psychological domain relates to 'body confidence' (*To what extent is it true for you . . . I would be confident about the appearance of my body when taking part in sport or exercise activity*). Figure 7.5 shows that nearly 4 out of 10 women say that this is *'somewhat untrue or not at all true'* for them. Only a quarter of all women express strong confidence in their body appearance in a sporting situation compared with 40 percent of men. This lack of confidence in body appearance in sporting situations is formed at a young age with the findings consistent with those found in other studies as discussed in Chapter 5. Figure 7.6 shows amongst young people aged between 16 to 25 years male confidence in their body image is very high but the picture is more mixed for women with 44 percent of 16 to 19-year-old women expressing some lack of confidence in their body appearance. Interestingly this proportion falls as young women move into their 20s but remains at about the 30 percent level and significantly above that of their male counterparts.

Another question in the psychological domain sought to establish how important sport was as part of a person's personal identity. It asked '*To*

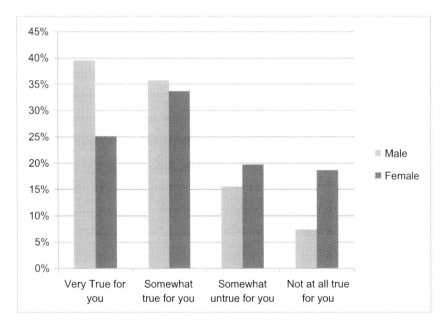

Figure 7.5 Body confidence by gender in the adult (16 plus) English population. 'To what extent is it true for you . . . I would be confident about the appearance of my body when taking part in sport or exercise activity'

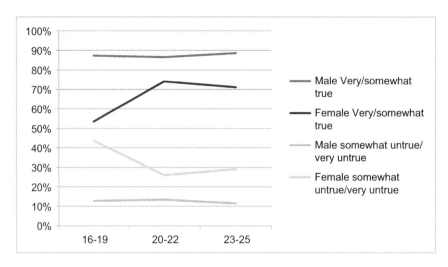

Figure 7.6 Body confidence amongst the young in the English population. 'To what extent is it true for you . . . I would be confident about the appearance of my body when taking part in sport or exercise activity'

what extent is it true for you . . . I would feel a real loss if I was forced to give up playing sport or from ever taking part in sport in the future.' Figure 7.7 shows how men and women responded to this question. Again there are marked differences with 44 percent of men saying this is very true for them compared with 28 percent of women. Perhaps of more concern is the large proportion, a third of women, at the other end of the spectrum who agreed that they would not feel any sense of loss if they were never able to play sport in the future.

However, as discussed earlier, it is not just in the psychological domain that we see gender differences. Answers to question items in both the physiological and social domains also demonstrate fundamental differences in how men and women relate to sport. For example one of the questions in the physiological domain explores perceived ability as follows: *'How would you rate yourself compared with people of your own age and gender . . . General sporting ability and skills'*. The framing of this question was purposely designed to provide a relative response with the use of the wording *'compared with people of your own age and gender'*. In an objectively rational world one would expect to see parity in the percentage of respondents who see themselves on the positive side of this balance sheet and those who see themselves on the negative side. And Figure 7.8 shows that this is exactly the profile that we get from the female respondents. However, the response from men is very different with many more seeing themselves as 'above average' than those seeing themselves as 'below

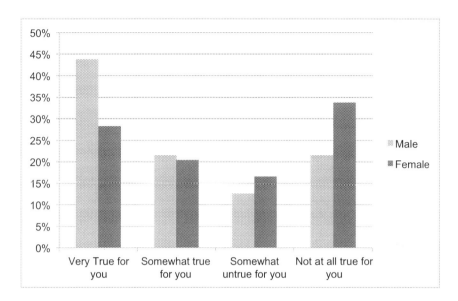

Figure 7.7 'Sporting identity' by gender in the adult (16 plus) English population. 'To what extent is it true for you . . . I would feel a real loss if I was forced to give up playing sport or from ever taking part in sport in the future'

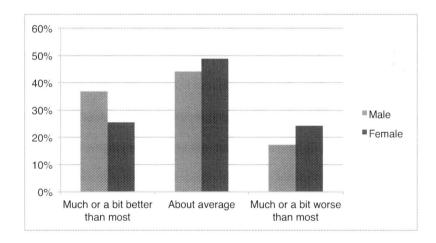

Figure 7.8 'Perceived sporting ability' by gender in the adult (16 plus) English population. How would you rate yourself compared with people of your own age and gender . . . 'General sporting ability and skills'

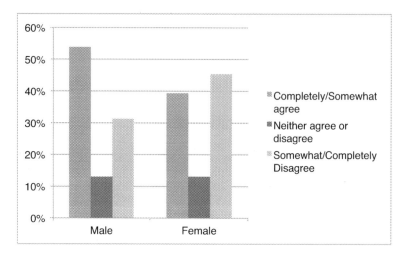

Figure 7.9 'Social connections in sport' in the adult (16 plus) English population by gender. 'To what extent do you agree ... Most of my friends regularly take part in sport'

average'. An objective observer might commend women on their rational and measured response to this question, but the reality is that the skewed positive response by men demonstrates a gendered advantage in the profile that in turn translates, through higher sporting capital scores, into higher probabilities of participating in sport.

A question item in the social domain also reveals enlightening gender differences that characterise relationships to sport. When asked *'To what extent do you agree . . . Most of my friends regularly take part in sport'* as shown in Figure 7.9, 54 percent of men *'completely agree'* compared with only 31 percent of women. With men having a higher probability of taking part in sport themselves, we might expect more men than women to have a more extensive network of friends that also take part. But the mere fact that men are much more likely than women to mix in social networks that have a positive relationship to sport increases their connections, familiarity and the normality of sport in their lives – all leading to increased probabilities of participating or of making a return to sport participation easier after a period of inactivity or drop out.

Sporting capital and social class – loading the dice for sports participation?

The focus of analysis so far has been on age and gender differences in the building blocks (question items and domains) that make up sporting capital. But as we have already seen in Chapter 6 sporting capital is not just structured by gender, it is also a product of where people sit within the social class hierarchies in English society. Without wanting to replicate the statistical analysis already presented for gender or to churn out lots of further empirical facts and figures, a few salient pieces of analysis have been selected that demonstrate the substantive structural class inequalities that characterise sport in England when viewed through a sporting capital lens and help us better understand the nature of these differences. Figure 7.10 shows how the probability of participating in sport changes with increases in sporting capital for 'upper' and 'lower' social class groups. It demonstrates that for any given level of sporting capital the probability of participating in sport is higher for the upper social class group than it is for the lower social class group. This suggests that the external barriers facing those from a lower social class background are greater and more difficult to overcome than those faced by their higher social class counterparts (see Chapter 3 for a discussion on the nature and impact of barriers).

Measuring inequities in participation between social class groups tells us about the outcome, but does little to help us better understand the causes. An examination of variations in the levels of sporting capital between different social class groups tells us something more profound about the underlying factors that lead to these inequities and the culture that shapes them. Analysis in Chapter 6 showed how the mean Sporting Capital Index scores are significantly higher for the upper social class

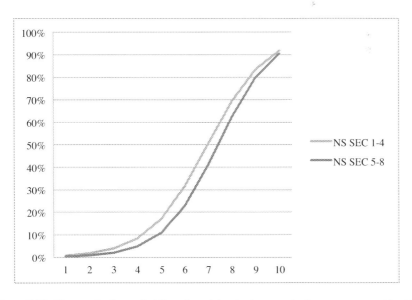

Figure 7.10 Changes in the probability of participating in sport (at least once a week) with changes in sporting capital – by social class. English adult (16 plus) population

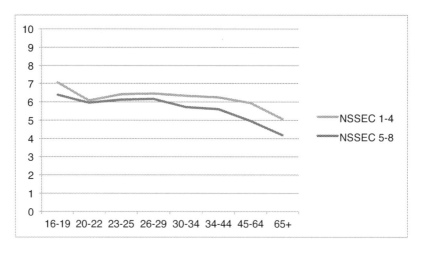

Figure 7.11 Changes in sporting capital mean scores with age and social class in the adult (16 plus) English population

group (NS-SEC 1–4) (6.0) than for the lower social class group (NS-SEC 5–8) (5.3). Figure 7.11 shows how the SCI scores change with age for both upper and lower social class groups. The highest sporting capital levels are found in 16 to 19-year-olds in the upper social class group (NS-SEC 1–4) with an average score of over 7. It is interesting to see that by the age of 22 years sporting capital levels converge as the upper social class group declines to meet that of the lower group. In later life, however, those in the upper social class group maintain sporting capital at higher levels than their lower social class counterparts.

Figure 7.12 provides a more in-depth analysis of how age interacts with social class to impact on levels of sporting capital. To enable analysis at this sub-group level the sporting capital scores have been shown using a collapsed 5-point scale derived from the 10-point SCI scale. In addition those scoring 1 and 2 on the 5-point scale have been combined to show those with low levels of sporting capital and those scoring 4 and 5 have been combined to show those with high levels. The results demonstrate how the proportions in the highest sporting capital group (scores of 4 and 5 combined) are greater for those in the upper social class groups at all ages and that the differences increase with age. Up to the age of 45 years the decline in sporting capital for those in the upper social class groups is a gradual one. This is in marked contrast to those in the lowest social class groups where sporting capital levels of those categorised as 4 and 5 drop rapidly after the age of 29 years.

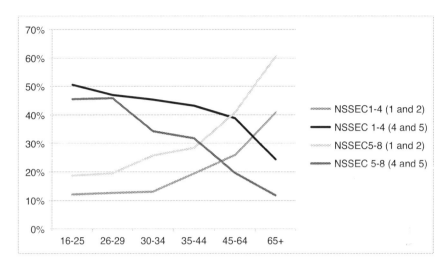

Figure 7.12 Changes in Sporting Capital Index (SCI) scores by age and social class in the adult (16 plus) English population. (Scores are on a collapsed 5-point scale with 1 and 2 combined (a low SCI score) and 4 and 5 combined (a high SCI score)

Figure 7.13 shows how domain scores, psychological, physiological and social, vary by social class. The patterns and differences we see in the profile across the domains bears remarkable similarities with those already presented for gender. In all three domains those in the higher social class group have significantly higher mean scores than those in the lowest social class group. Again the psychological domain receives the lowest mean ratings and also shows the greatest disparities between different social class groups.

An interesting measure in the social domain concerns how confident and at ease a person feels when they are in situations where people take part in sport or exercise activity. This relates more broadly to how inviting or intimidating people are likely to see sport environments such as gyms, sports centres and swimming pools. Figure 7.14 shows that there are disparities in how people relate to the environments in which sport takes place as a consequence of a person's social class. Just over 50 percent of those in the upper social class group expressed a very positive view compared with 38 percent of those in the lowest social class group.

Another measure in the social domain looks at how 'sporty' a person's friendship networks are by asking '*To what extent do you agree . . . Most of*

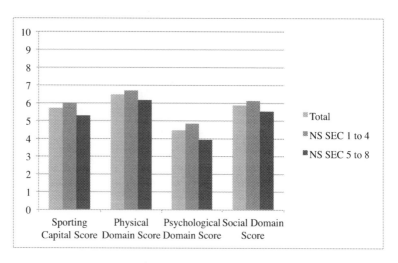

Figure 7.13 Mean domain scores (on a scale of 1 to 10 with 1 low and 10 high) by gender in the adult (16 plus) English population

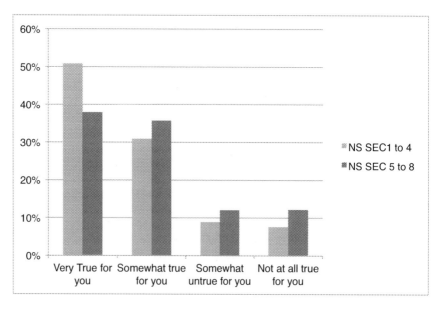

Figure 7.14 'Self confidence in sporty situations' by social class in the adult (16 plus) English population. 'To what extent is it true for you ... I feel completely confident and at ease in situations where people take part in sport or exercise activity'

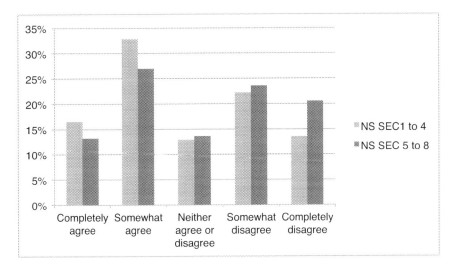

Figure 7.15 'Social connections to sport' by social class in the adult (16 plus) English population. 'To what extent do you agree ... Most of my friends regularly take part in sport'

my friends regularly take part in sport'. Figure 7.15 shows that the answer to this question is also socially skewed with those in the upper social class group much more likely to express a positive view on this measure than those in the lowest social class group. In fact over one in five of those in NS-SEC 5–8 completely disagreed with this statement compared with less than one in seven of those in NS-SEC 1–4. This raises particular concerns as it points towards the reinforcing nature of sporting capital both in a positive and negative sense. Someone who mixes with people who are sporty will , all other things being equal, be more likely to take part in sport themselves both because on a practical level they will have greater possibilities of finding someone to play with but also more subtly they will be influenced by the positive value systems that their friends demonstrate in relation to sport participation. Additionally people with higher levels of sporting capital (and higher scores on the social domain that contributes towards overall sporting capital levels) will by participating be likely to meet more people who play sport and as a consequence extend their friendship networks amongst sport participants. By definition this further builds their levels of sporting capital. Of course the opposite will also occur with fewer 'sporty friends' reinforcing values that are non-sporty and in turn increasing the probability of inactivity and further diminishing levels of sporting capital creating the conditions for a negative downward cycle.

Sporting capital and sporting preferences

In Chapter 6 I showed how the probability of participating in sport is directly related to levels of sporting capital. However, it is also reasonable to assume that levels of sporting capital will have some influence on both the frequency of participation in sport and the types of sport people choose to play. The theory suggests that the higher the levels of sporting capital the greater the motivation to participate and the greater potential to have a positive experience from that participation. This in turn is likely to increase the frequency of participation, although at some point one would assume that marginal returns in relation to enjoyment gained combined with external barriers of for example price, accessibility and other demands on time including work and family would ultimately constrain participation frequency amongst even the greatest enthusiasts with the most positive sporting capital profile. Figure 7.16 shows how the probability of participating in sport at different frequencies (at least once a month; at least once a week; and at least 3 times a week) changes with increasing levels of sporting capital. The shape of the probabilities is very different for each frequency of participating. As we would expect the probability of participating at least once a month starts to increase at much lower levels of sporting capital than the higher participation frequencies.

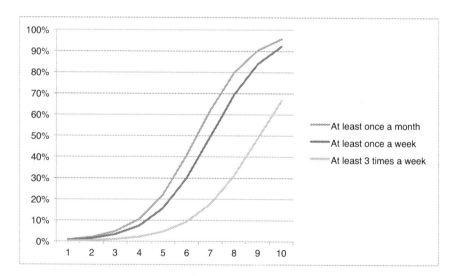

Figure 7.16 Probability of participating in sport for different frequencies with changes in the Sporting Capital Index score (1 is low and 10 is high) in the adult (16 plus) English population

At a Sporting Capital Index score of 6 the probability of participating at least once a month is 41 percent, which compares with a probability of 30 percent for those participating at least once a week and only 9 percent for those participating at least 3 times a week. The shape of the curves for both the lower frequency rates of at least once a month and at least once a week pick up steeply from a Sporting Capital Index score of 4 to 5 and peak at over 90 percent probability of participating at the highest level of sporting capital. However, the shape of the curve for those participating at the high frequency of at least 3 times a week is very different with a much more gradual increase in the probability of participating at these frequencies with increases in sporting capital. In fact up to a Sporting Capital Index score of 5 the probability of participating at least 3 times a week is negligible and, interestingly, even at a maximum sporting capital score of 10 the probability of participating at this frequency peaks at 67 percent. This supports the argument that even amongst the most highly sporting literate, confident and connected individuals, there is a ceiling or limit to how much sport people want to play or are able to negotiate and manage in the context of their life circumstances.

Turning to the types of sporting preferences associated with different levels of sporting capital, it seems reasonable to assume that there would be some kind of relationship between the two. I discussed in Chapter 1 how use of the word 'sport' as a collective noun tends to oversimplify the wide diversity of activities that it encompasses. This diversity spans across different physical challenges of for example hand eye coordination, dexterity, strength, speed, flexibility, body contact and aggression; to different social and organisational contexts for example between individual activities, team events, levels of competition, levels of formality or informality, interaction with the natural or man-made and built environments. In turn different sports can pose different psychological challenges for the individual in terms of their impact on and interaction with personal identity, self efficacy and self confidence. Put simply, there is a world of difference, albeit they all fit within the same broad typology, between the challenges and experiences of for example, playing golf with its high technical requirement, its social context that requires both knowledge of written rules of the game and unwritten rules of the social world in which it is played, compared with playing rugby union with its own social norms, team ethic, high intensity and physicality. These two sports again provide very different experiences and challenges to those of taking part in say informal recreational swimming, or going for a leisurely cycle ride with the family or visiting the gym.

Figure 7.17 shows how the relationship between sporting capital and participating in sport varies by different type of sports. Sports have been grouped into broad categories of 'Team', 'Individual', 'Racquet', Water'

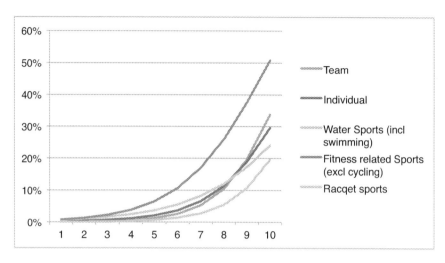

Figure 7.17 Probability of participating by type of sport (at least once a month) with changes in the Sporting Capital Index score (1 is low and 10 is high) in the English adult (16 plus) population

(including swimming) and 'Health and fitness related' activities (excluding walking). (see Nordern, 2013). The results show an interesting variation in the profile by the type of sport and suggest that:

- Fitness-related sports provide a higher probability of attracting those on the lowest sporting capital levels into sport (i.e. those with Sporting Capital Index scores of between 3 and 6) than other types of sport. Conversely there are smaller relative returns to be gained for fitness-related sports' participation from incremental increases in sporting capital levels at the higher end of the spectrum (8, 9 and 10) than there are for other types of sports.

- With the probability of participating in team, individual and racquet sports so low up to a sporting capital level of 6 or 7, the biggest gains for these sports are to be achieved by increasing sporting capital levels between 8 and 10. The profile for racquet sports is a particularly challenging one with the biggest relative gains to be achieved, a doubling of the probability of participating from 10 percent to 20 percent, by moving from a sporting capital score of 9 to one of 10.

Figure 7.18 examines changes in the probabilities of participating with changing levels of sporting capital for two of our largest participant sports, cycling and swimming. Although both sports show very small gains in the

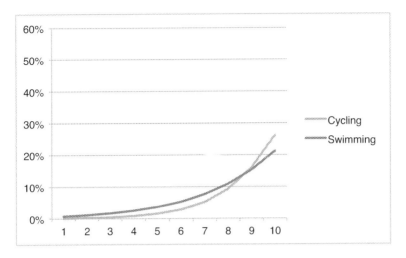

Figure 7.18 Probability of participating in swimming and cycling (at least once a month) with changes in the Sporting Capital Index score (1 is low and 10 is high) in the English adult (16 plus) population

probability of participating with increasing sporting capital levels from 1 to 3, both show a steady increase with sporting capital increases from 4 upwards. However, the results suggest greater relative gains in participation for cycling than swimming with increasing sporting capital scores from 6 upwards.

The above analysis has focused on how the probabilities of participating in different types of sport change with changes in levels of sporting capital. Another way of looking at this is to examine how the sporting capital profiles for different sports vary across the adult population in England. Figure 7.19 shows the profile for different groups of sports and separately for cycling and swimming. Because of the sample sizes, it was necessary to collapse the Sporting Capital Index scores from a 10-point scale to a 5-point scale. This analysis is revealing as it shows how for all sports the highest proportions taking part are those with a sporting capital level of 4 out of 5, making up between 40 and 50 percent of all participants across all sports groups. However, perhaps of more interest is the predominance of participants with high levels of sporting capital in Team and Racquet sports when compared to Individual and Fitness-related activities. For example 82 percent of all Team sport participants and 79 percent of Racquet sport participants have sporting capital levels of 4 and 5 compared with 68 percent in Individual sports, 55 percent in Water Sports and 55 percent in Swimming.

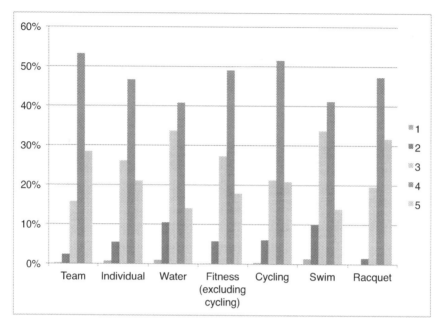

Figure 7.19 Distribution of sporting capital levels across different types of sport (on a scale of 1 is low and 5 is high) in the English adult (16 plus) population

Summary and implications

The last two chapters have been different in style and layout to those that preceded them. They have presented the outcomes from an empirical study which translates sporting capital into a measurable, quantifiable scale of attributes or characteristics that can be attached to an individual and aggregated to a nation. This quantification will inevitably be challenged by some who consider that the mere process of seeking to measure such complex phenomena is epistemologically unsound. And I would agree that there is some validity to this argument, although it is one that could equally be applied to any field of empirical study in the social sciences and if adhered to would rule out a wide discipline of quantitative studies that have contributed to our knowledge and understanding of human behaviour and the contexts in which it takes place. The relative merit of quantitative versus qualitative research is not a debate to have here. In defence of the methods employed and their validity I would say the following: 1) that this is exploratory research which applies a systematic and sophisticated approach to quantifying the theory of sporting capital to a large population study. It was supported by large sample sizes and random sampling procedures but was an approach constrained by the resources and survey platform available at the time; 2) the general patterns and relationships established are consistent and credible and provide substantive insights that increase our knowledge and understanding of community sport behaviours, and the processes and mechanisms that shape them; 3) the results of this study support and add weight to the theory of sporting capital as a paradigm shift in thinking for public policy; and 4) this is the beginning and not the end of a research process. The methods are capable of replication to provide benchmarks for change and comparison whether that is at a national or international level or local project intervention level. There is also the opportunity for further research to refine the methods and to combine qualitative and quantitative research designs to better understand the nature of sporting capital, how it is formed, the contexts which influence it and its relationships to behaviour change and maintenance. This is a discussion I return to in the final chapter of this book.

What are the most important findings that we can take away from this empirical study of sporting capital in England? I would summarise them as follows:

- **Structural inequalities in sporting capital.** The levels of sporting capital an individual has is not down to random luck or chance. There are structural relationships associated with age, gender and social class that determine an individual's life chances in sport. Sporting capital decreases with age although it is more durable than sports participation; it is substantially higher amongst men than women with the gap at its greatest in the youngest age groups and then decreases into middle and older age; the sporting capital gap between those in the upper and lower social class groups is broadly equivalent in scale to the gap between the genders.
- **Sporting capital and gender.** Given the longstanding inequities in participation in sport between men and women it is not surprising to find that these are also seen in relation to levels of sporting capital. However, the fact that gender differences in sporting capital occur at a young age and persist throughout the life-course provides us with a greater insight into the underlying causes of these inequities than can be provided by a focus on participation behaviours alone. There is nothing about sporting capital that would point towards any pre-existing genetic advantage or disadvantage that is gender related. We are all born with a sporting capital clean sheet. The gender inequities in sporting capital are therefore a reflection of the wider cultural context and early socialisation processes that shape and define men and women's relationship to sport. And these gender differences run deep. The evidence would suggest that lower levels of sporting capital amongst women are shaped by lower scores in all three domains, psychological, social and

physiological. The differences are reflected in answers to the individual question items when we delve deeper to explore the building blocks that make up the domains such as body confidence, perceived ability and the sportiness of friendship networks. Put simply, on average women are much more likely to see themselves as less sporty than men, to have lower self confidence in their physical abilities, to feel less confident in sporting situations and are less likely to mix in sporting social networks. The evidence also suggests that inequities in sporting capital are magnified for women in the lower social class groups.

If public policy is to be successful in narrowing the gender gap in sports participation, it must address and narrow the underlying gender gap in sporting capital. Women may face particular challenges in relation to the external barriers to participation such as price, accessibility and time constraints and addressing these would help reduce the gap. But it can only go so far. The most impact will be made by addressing those underlying factors that more directly impact on sporting capital formation and maintenance. These are often more about the subtleties of how sporting opportunities are provided rather than simply the quantity and accessibility of opportunities. In the earliest years of sporting capital formation the family environment is crucial. But from a public policy perspective the biggest opportunity to build sporting capital and to narrow gender inequities is in primary and early secondary school years with a focus on providing an education that helps form positive attitudes and values towards sport and recreational physical activity amongst both boys and girls. In the community all the key players, including local authorities, national governing bodies and their voluntary sports club networks, must focus on providing a quality sporting experience that empowers women to express themselves physically by first attracting them into sport and then providing an environment that reinforces and builds sporting capital rather than one that inexorably chips away and diminishes it until drop out and disenchantment is the inevitable consequence.

- **Sporting capital and social class.** Participation rates in sport are socially skewed towards the upper social class groups and have been for as long as measures of sports participation have been in place. However, the way social class interacts with sport to shape and influence the experience, perceptions, attitudes, values and ultimately participation behaviours of individuals is complex and as a consequence will not respond to simplistic public policy 'solutions'. The default assumption is that people in the lower social class groups participate less because they face more challenging external factors including lack of access, cost, transport difficulties, longer, more unsociable and less reliable hours of work, and particular demands of childcare. There is truth in this assumption but it does not paint the complete picture. The results of this empirical study show that there are more fundamental processes at work that lead not only to inequities in participation but also to inequities in levels of sporting capital. As with gender, these inequities are deep rooted, start at an early age and span all three domains and many of the key building-block measures of self confidence, ability and social connections that go to make them up. The results would suggest that although it has an important place in public policy intervention, barrier reduction alone will not overcome social class differences in participation in sport and that to be successful sports development policy and practice needs to address the more fundamental antecedents of low participation rates stemming from inequities in the levels of sporting capital across different social class groups. To do this will require a re-examination of early years learning experiences in the family and in pre-school environments, sport pedagogy in the education system, the nature and style of traditional sport delivery systems including in sports clubs and community sport facilities, and better targeting of interventions with more sophisticated approaches to sports development and outreach that combine barrier reduction with sporting capital enhancement tailored to the particular needs of the individual.

- **Sporting capital and sporting preferences.** The results from this empirical study show that there are differences in the relationship between levels of sporting capital and the frequency and types of sport people take part in. All frequencies and all sports have one thing in common, as sporting capital levels increase the probability of participating increases and vice versa. As we might expect, however, those with the highest frequency of participation have the highest levels of sporting capital. This finding is important for public policy as it enables us to say with some degree of confidence that not only will we get more people participating in sport with increases in sporting capital but we will also get more people participating more frequently. This has particular relevance for public policy in health where higher frequencies of participation are related to enhanced health outcomes. However, the results also show how challenging it is to increase the number of those participating in sport at very high frequencies and points towards the need for a broad agenda for health promotion that combines sport development with wider physical activity and lifestyle change.

The relationship between sporting capital and the probability of participating in different types of sports raises interesting questions about the nature of those sports and how they are provided. We can see from the results that fitness-related sports are potentially much more attractive as an entry point into sport for those on low levels of sporting capital than are team and racquet sports. Why, however, should this be the case? It may be that some sports are inherently more demanding on sporting capital than other sports; many fitness-related sports have few technical demands, can be taken part in casually and require little organisation. However, sports like golf, tennis and rugby union and league are very technically demanding, have strong social and institutional structures and can be very competitive. The results would suggest that sports like these, unless they can make significant innovative changes to the way they are structured and delivered to make them more like fitness-related activities, are misdirecting their energies in trying to recruit participants with sporting capital levels of 5 or less. The national governing bodies of these sports have a particular vested interest in finding ways to raise overall sporting capital, particularly amongst the young, through providing more attractive junior schemes and working cooperatively with schools and colleges. Many need to go beyond this to change the culture of how they are provided and operated to make them less threatening for people on low levels of sporting capital and to change the way sport is presented and coached in community settings. Without these kinds of changes these types of sports will always be consigned to competing with each other for a small minority market of the 'very sporty' (the 20 percent with sporting capital levels of 8, 9 or 10) in the population.

Chapter 8

Building sporting capital

Applying the theory to policy and practice

Introduction

In this book I have introduced a new theoretical perspective for community sports development, the theory of sporting capital, which values and emphasises individual capacity-building while acknowledging societal and contextual influences on the nature and extent of those capacities. Without in any way seeking to minimise the challenges or to suggest easy solutions, I have taken an optimistic normative position that public policy delivered in the right way and in the right context can make a difference to increase the potential for engagement in sport and through sport achieve wider social, economic and health outcomes. By implication I have suggested that even with the best of intentions the way public policy has been conceived to date with its lack of a coherent theoretical foundation has limited its impact on achieving its ambitions for community sport. In response I have suggested that the theory of sporting capital creates the opportunity for a paradigm shift in the way public policy is conceived and framed to provide a new lens on the mechanisms and processes that impact on individual propensities to take part in sport. I have emphasised how viewing public policy through the prism of sporting capital, dispersed into its three constituent domains, can unlock individual potential to take part in sport, can build capacities where they are lacking and can take a more socially nuanced and sophisticated approach to addressing 'wicked problems' that require a synthesis of disciplines and intervention approaches. I have suggested that the insight provided by sporting capital theory not only increases the chances of transformational change in sports participation but by placing sport in the family of 'capitals' that includes social, cultural and human capital, it increases the chances of sport contributing to wider social change.

The empirical evidence presented in the previous two chapters paints a unique and insightful picture of community sport in England. It shows how the landscape of community sport is characterised not just by inequalities in the distribution of sporting behaviours across society but by more fundamental structural inequalities in the distribution of the capital that supports and drives those behaviours. A sceptical reader might think that this is hardly a new finding, hardly surprising and perhaps would even go so far as to suggest that it is just reaffirming the obvious. However, I would contend that the landscape of English sport painted in the previous chapters although perhaps not a surprise to those with a sociological imagination (Mills, 1959), which by definition includes many in the academic world, has not been obvious to most, if not all of those administrators and politicians, nationally and locally, who have held the public purse strings for sports development over the last 40 years. The general position taken by the latter has been one dominated by the pervasive idea that the lack of progress in growing participation numbers and inability to shift stubborn structural inequalities associated with age, gender and social class has been primarily a function of inequality of 'opportunity' and not of inequality of 'desire', 'choice' and 'motivation' underpinned by inequalities of sporting capital. The implication is that what stops people taking part in sport is primarily things that are external to them, things such as lack of time, insufficient access to facilities, inadequate childcare, too high prices. The response has invariably been an emphasis on supply side interventions, concessionary pricing policies and traditional views about sport that emphasise competition and the power and leverage of major events. Such a conclusion and response is perhaps not surprising from a political perspective as it frames the problem in a way that seems straightforward and tangible. Buildings are solid and can easily be counted; local price concessions create political capital and can easily be associated with certain ideological perspectives; increasing opportunities for competitive sport in and between schools seems to many a self evident good thing; investing huge sums in major events with a promise of participation legacies suits many interest groups even where there is at best a limited evidence base to support such outcomes.

It is the less tangible nature of sporting capital, I would contend, that has made it less amenable to public policy priority. Of course the use of the term 'sporting capital' is not required for elements of past public policy to have reflected some of the principles embedded in the theory. It could be argued, and I would be supportive of this view, that some of the shift in strategic thinking in the late 1980s and early 1990s (see Houlihan and White, 2002) that initiated the sports development profession and was reflected in people-oriented outreach programmes like 'Action Sport' and the 'Active Communities Development Fund' resonated with elements of sporting capital theory, if not presented in those terms. The social marketing efforts in programmes such as '50 plus and all to play for', 'Ever Thought of Sport', 'What's your Sport?' and 'What's on for Women' included, albeit variably, some elements of sporting capital in their thinking but failed to make any sustained impact due to their often somewhat simplistic assumptions of human behaviour and associated triggers of behaviour change. As Mike

Collins the then Head of Research at the G.B. Sports Council said, "I believe any campaign should relate to the strategy and be sports development led otherwise the dog gets wagged by the 'public affairs' tail and the lure of sponsorship and the needs of sponsors" (Collins, 1988). Even if the campaigns pressed some of the right buttons, they were invariably literally or at least metaphorically invisible to those who were antagonistic or at best apathetic to their messages.

More recently the Sport England programme 'This Girl Can' (Sport England, 2017) has been credited with some success at attracting disenchanted young women back into sport. And the title of the campaign shows how it links into the psychological domain to address the lack of self confidence and self efficacy characteristic of many young women's experience of sport. To quote the Sport England Chief Executive Jennie Price,

> Before we began this campaign, we looked very carefully at what women were saying about why they felt sport and exercise was not for them. Some of the issues, like time and cost, were familiar, but one of the strongest themes was a fear of judgement. Worries about being judged for being the wrong size, not fit enough and not skilled enough came up time and again.
>
> (Sport England, 2017)

The verdict is still out as to whether such campaign messages pitched at a national level, although focused on a key aspect of sporting capital, can be translated beyond short-term impacts to achieve sustained behaviour change. Cavill and Baumann (2004, p. 787), reviewing the experience from mass media physical activity campaigns concluded that,

> Beyond increasing awareness, the effects of campaigns are less clear. At the next level in the model, we found limited data to indicate the ability of campaigns to lead to changes in knowledge, beliefs or understanding of key aspects of the physical activity message.

We have seen in earlier chapters how an individual's relationship to sport in psychological and physical terms is strongly embedded in their sense of self from a very young age and reinforced by their social connections through their formative years and into adulthood and older age. To assume that young women on low levels of sporting capital can be enthused by a public policy message to kick start the process of building their sporting capital to levels that will encourage and sustain a long-term commitment to sport is a very big ask. The evidence from previous campaigns would suggest that any direct success attributable to campaign intervention will, where achieved, be amongst those with medium to medium-high levels of sporting capital rather than those with the low to very low levels where the 'leap to participate' is too big a chasm to cross on the basis of such generic messages. As Cavill and Baumann (2004, p. 787) conclude in their review of the impact of mass media physical activity campaigns,

> It is interesting to note the changes in physical activity reported among some sub-groups of the population. At each stage in the campaign process there is a drop-out effect, as people fail to see the campaign, don't understand it, decide not to register, and so on. The small sub-group that remains at the end of the process is likely to consist of people who are motivated to become more physically active, and changes among such people are likely.

Sporting capital: a strategic 'game changer'

I have positioned sporting capital as a universal theory that is not constrained in its relevance by temporal experience. As a consequence I would rather not limit the reference framework for public policy critique to current policy frameworks or current community sport programmes. I will leave it to others to carry out such critical analysis. I have already indicated that in the framing of the 'This Girl Can' campaign programme there is a resonance with sporting capital theory. However, selecting one programme is to perhaps miss the strategic point that sporting capital is a coherent holistic theory that in turn requires a coherent holistic strategic response. So rather than critique elements of current strategy I have set out below a positive vision of the key ingredients I would expect to see in a national sport strategy informed and shaped by sporting capital theory.

Firstly, a strategy built around the theory of sporting capital rather than seeking to achieve *'sport for all'* with its participation focus would have as its vision *'sporting capital for all'* with its individual capacity-building focus. A sporting capital-led strategy would have a vision of increasing sporting capital across the population and of reducing the inequities in its distribution across different groups in the population including by age, gender, class, ethnicity and disability. This is far from a subtle shift. The emphasis given by the idea of sport for all and its variants to include setting ambitious targets to increase sustained participation rates in sport is an unrealistic one focused on behavioural outcomes rather than the behavioural capacities that lie at the heart of sporting capital theory. There will never be a society in which everyone regularly participates in sport throughout the whole of their life-course. However, building the capacity of all individuals to participate in sport supported by appropriate opportunities is more philosophically sound and realistic if still a hugely challenging one for public policy. Of course the outcome from increased sporting capital across the population would be more people regularly participating in sport. But in a strategy focused on sporting capital the emphasis would be focused on the causes or antecedents to participation rather than the behavioural outcomes themselves characterised as they are by temporal vagaries and potentially misleading interpretations. The judgement of success would not be on the rates of participation at any given time, impacted as they are by seasonality, the weather conditions, economic conditions and personal life circumstances, but by the more stable measure of sporting capital growth and distribution.

Secondly, a sporting capital-led strategy would have a coherent and connected narrative that would view the community sport system as a complex but interconnected set of agents and agencies contextualised by wider social and economic power relations and characterised by differential access to resources and spheres of influence. The strategy would identify the key agencies such as national governing bodies of sport, local authorities, schools, further and higher education establishments, county sport partnerships, social enterprises, charities, other third sector organisations and the private sector and assess how they interact with and influence the sporting capital levels of their constituents, members or customers. It would encourage agencies to explore their strengths and limitations and very importantly it would help them understand within a common model and linguistic framework where they fit in, what they can do best and how they are contributing towards a shared outcome of increasing sporting capital in the individuals and communities with which they interact. The common currency of 'sporting capital' across all agencies would encourage cooperation to build a sport literate, self confident, socially connected population. Where in the past there may have been competition for a small participant base characterised by drop out, churn and instability, a focus on sporting capital would encourage a climate of shared interests and cooperation across agencies transcending the temporal variability associated with participation behaviours albeit it recognising the causal link to them. This is to view sporting capital as the 'glue' that helps build partnerships within a framework of common purpose and shared interests.

The agents of change are the people who work in the sport system (inside the agencies referred to above) such as politicians, national sports administrators, academics, school teachers, nursery teachers, sports development officers, coaches, outreach and community workers, facility managers and sport volunteers. Sporting capital theory would again operate as a shared foundation for their work, providing a common language and sense of purpose. At a political level the prospect that a paradigm shift in the way sport policy is conceived and delivered that could break through the inertia of stagnating participation rates would appeal across the political spectrum. The philosophical positioning of sporting capital offers the potential for a consensus, valuing individual choice, freedom, empowerment, quality of life and well-being whilst acknowledging structural social and economic inequalities that crosses political and ideological boundaries. The potential for the transferability of capitals to deliver wider social, health and economic outcomes through sport would have a broad political appeal. At a practical level the strategy would promote shared understanding amongst the different agents of change, the sporting workforce, by supporting common learning and curriculum content tailored to the needs of each constituent group. In academia sporting capital theory within a framework of healthy critical debate could provide a foundation for course content in supporting a new generation of 'sporting capital literate' sports development professionals and would support a shared research agenda that crossed and integrated disciplines. Within facility management and health and fitness vocations, sporting capital could provide core curriculum content supported and promoted by professional membership associations. Amongst those agents whose primary focus is not sport but who have objectives that overlap with sport and or see sport as an instrument of social change, sporting capital could provide a language that would resonate well with their core business and help to build bridges across professions, vocations and disciplines. This includes those who work in health promotion, general practitioners, youth workers and youth offending, social work and social care.

The strategy would set targets based on increasing levels of sporting capital across the population and reducing the inequitable distribution of sporting capital amongst different sub-groups in the population. It would make tactical decisions on priority markets balancing social justice outcomes with cost effectiveness and realism on return on investment taking a wide social balance sheet perspective. The markets would be identified in relation to their level of sporting capital intersected with standard demographics of age, gender, class, ethnicity and disability. But beyond this, the strategy would take a life-stage approach to identify markets in key transition periods, at times of high risk of drop out, and the times when the opportunities for re-engagement are at their greatest. The evidence would suggest that the greatest potential returns in terms of participation in sport would be to focus efforts on those in the mid range levels of sporting capital where for example a significant shift in the number of people moving from a sporting capital level of 5 to levels 6 and 7 would pay large dividends in terms of increased probabilities of sustained regular participation in sport. Within this target market sustaining and re-engaging participants may for some only require behavioural 'nudges' that make sport easier or create better opportunities for positive experiences. Undoubtedly, a strategic debate would be required to examine how much resource should be focused on the 'low sporting capital market' where change would be more difficult to achieve and where the returns, at least measured in relation to sport participation, would be marginal. The debate at this end of the sporting capital market place would almost certainly focus on the physical activity and health end of the policy spectrum and the potential returns from a broader health and social balance sheet perspective.

A strategy with sporting capital at its core would look for an appropriate balance between investment in barrier and constraint reduction, opportunity creation and individual capacity building. The outcome would, however, be conceived consistently across all of these areas of public intervention in terms of building the stock of sporting capital. As we have seen in earlier chapters, it is a mistake to consider these elements of the sports system as in any way independent or mutually exclusive. An individual's stock of sporting capital is a function of education, knowledge and lived experiences. All of these take place in different settings and the nature and quality of these settings is crucial. For example, a quality-built sporting environment that is easy to get to and where the physical fabric is 'fit for purpose' is architecturally and aesthetically pleasing, and is stimulating yet comfortable will help to sustain participation and build sporting capital. An environment that is inaccessible, dark, and dingy, with badly designed sports spaces and surfaces and with the perception, if not the reality, of being unsafe will over time reduce sporting capital and the motivation to participate. However, the nature of the setting is not just a function of the physical fabric, it is as much if not more about the interaction with people, the staff and volunteers that run a facility or manage an outdoor environment and with fellow participants, in terms of shared social norms and ways of behaving that make an individual feel comfortable and welcomed or ill at ease and intimidated. A strategy focused around building sporting capital will see investment in opportunity creation as a means to unlock participation behaviours from the existing stock of sporting capital. However, it will recognise that in isolation a policy focus on access to quality buildings and lower prices will appeal to those with high sporting capital but will not reach the very large numbers in the population whose sporting capital is below the threshold where simple reduction in external barriers motivates participation. For these people, successful intervention requires more sophisticated and challenging approaches to both reach and attract them and to sustain their engagement. In their cases the styles of delivery tailored to their level of sporting capital become crucial. Such intervention approaches are discussed in more detail later in this chapter and in Chapter 9.

A strategy structured around sporting capital theory would, as discussed above, include remedial approaches focused on building and sustaining sporting capital across different life-stages. However, the theory and the supporting evidence review carried out in Chapter 5 point emphatically towards the importance of early learning experiences in the formation of sporting capital and how these experiences track over time into later life. Although the returns would not be felt in the short term, it would be inconceivable that a strategy with a central aim of increasing sporting capital across the population would not prioritise interventions focused on young people. Of course this is not a new perspective, and the current Government strategy for sport (H.M. Government, 2015) and Sport England's strategy

(Sport England, 2016) have emphasised the importance of reaching and influencing young people. A recent report by UK Active, 'Start Young and Stay Active' (undated, p. 6) has emphasised the importance of childhood physical literacy and called, "on (the) government to recognise the unique position of parents in sustaining an active household and to implement programmes which enable new parents to have the knowledge and support to do this." The Youth Sport Trust in collaboration with Sport England and a range of other partners including a number of national governing bodies of sport has published a 'Primary School Physical Literacy Framework', (Youth Sport Trust, undated) that "has been designed to support those working in primary schools to consider how best they can structure their PE and school sport provision to ensure maximum opportunity is provided to develop the physical literacy of all their pupils". The Youth Sport Trust has also published an 'Early Years Physical Literacy Framework (Youth Sport Trust, 2017) that supports the 2011 Chief Medical Officer (CMO) recommendations for levels of physical activity for 0–5-year-olds (Department of Health, 2011).

The above developments reflect a growing realisation in public policy of the importance of early years' experience on later life participation in sport and physical activity The difference in a sporting capital-led strategy would be in the level of priority and attention given to this target market, the forms the interventions take and the determination to reach and influence the very young pre-school population. The evidence suggests that the factors that influence a child's relationship to sport start the day they are born. Parents and families have a significant formative influence on the value system and social norms that promote an active lifestyle and on what are considered gender appropriate behaviours. Although sports development does not have a direct relationship with pre-school children and their parents, it certainly has a stake in this population. A sporting capital-led strategy would look for effective partnerships with agencies and professionals that can reach and impact on pre-school children's learning experiences, including those working in health care, nursery schools, other children and family services and through children's centres created as part of the 'Sure Start' programmes focused on 0 to 4-year-olds in disadvantaged areas (see Bouchal, P. and Norris, E., undated). Sport literacy and learning in primary schools would be prioritised within a sporting capital-focused strategy with support for primary school teachers on curriculum content and materials. This support would go beyond light touch advocacy to include government set standards of achievement to attach the same priority to physical literacy outcomes as to reading, writing and numeracy. The strategy would strengthen support to stakeholder groups focused on promoting and resourcing more specialist physical education teachers in primary school settings and providing them with support materials that encourage motor skill development and positive attitudes towards physical activity. Examples of the kinds of interventions and guidance materials targeted at the very young are provided by experience in the United States with the work of 'Shape America' (the Society of Health and Physical Educators) with its mission to "advance professional practice and promote research related to health and physical education, physical activity, dance, and sport" (Shape America, undated); the 'eXtension Alliance for Better Child Care' (eXtension Alliance for Better Childcare, undated) and the 'Let's Move! Childcare' programme (Lets Move! Child Care undated).

The strategy would explicitly address structural inequalities in the distribution of sporting capital by targeting disadvantaged social groups. It would in particular focus interventions on those target markets where socio-economic circumstances are compounded by the intersection of class and gender and class and ethnicity. It would be acknowledged that addressing deficits in sporting capital in these target markets poses particular challenges on resources and potential returns on investment. It would recognise the need to concentrate investment and not to attempt to spread it too thinly. In the case of social class inequalities the evidence suggests that external constraints play a more influential role than it does for the more affluent socially advantaged population. As a consequence opportunity creation has an important role to play in poorer more disadvantaged neighbourhoods. This must not distract, however, from the deep-rooted inequities in sporting capital that impact on the lower social class groups across all ages and both genders. Targeting the roots of these inequalities through early learning and socialisation processes would be prioritised in a sporting capital-focused strategy. Although not addressed in this book, building sporting capital amongst the disabled population would be a priority although more research is required to better understand how sporting capital operates amongst disabled populations and the ways in which it may need to be re-framed and applied in this context.

A sporting capital-led strategy would pose particular challenges to the national governing bodies of sport. The evidence shows that a traditional sport offer with its formal structures, rules, conditions of play and social norms limits its attraction and appeal to a very large segment of the population on lower levels of sporting capital. National governing bodies would need to review and assess their sport in this context and set strategic priorities on their target markets and how they shape and develop their offer in response. It may be legitimate for a sport to define its core market as those with higher levels of sporting capital and to focus its efforts to better appeal to this core market to improve the quality of experience to sustain engagement and extend its growth. National funding programmes should not force sports into unrealistic ambitions in markets where they are unappealing and doomed to relative failure. Notwithstanding, sports should be challenged to consider opportunities where they can push their comfort zone and their traditional market boundaries to seek ways to reach and appeal to those with sporting capital levels that lie outside of their natural constituencies. The levers available to them include adapted forms of their sports with in particular modified sports for young people and veterans and people with varying levels of ability; working to make sports clubs more accessible and welcoming; supporting community coach education and outreach; and strengthening links with primary and secondary schools.

The strategy would discuss and explore the relationship between sporting capital and other wider social, economic and health outcomes through a sophisticated understanding of how these different capitals are formed, the relationship between them and how they may be made more 'transferable'. In this context sport could be transformed in language and presentation from a peripheral and second class citizen in social policy to one of centrality and equivalence. The relationships with key agencies outside of sport would be set out supported by a coherent and evidence-based case for the potential of sport to deliver wider returns on investment as part of a family of 'capitals' that enhance quality of life, individual and societal well-being.

Finally, the strategy would be informed by a programme of ongoing research that would build on the empirical study already presented in this book to extend it to new quantitative and qualitative approaches that provide insight about sporting capital formation, maintenance and growth. Academic experts would be encouraged to combine with policy makers and practitioners to develop a programme of collaborative cross and interdisciplinary research. Encouragement would be given for international comparative research with opportunities for debate and shared learning. The theory would be constantly challenged and tested in a transparent way that emphasised continuous learning and innovation. An approach to intervention-based evaluation discussed in the final chapter would be taken. New innovative approaches particularly targeted at hard to reach populations and designed to overcome structural inequalities in sporting capital would be trialled and evaluated. The judgement of success would be on target markets reached, sporting capital change achieved and where applicable wider outcomes delivered through the transferability of capitals. The emphasis would be on processes, mechanisms, impact, learning, replicability and context.

Sporting capital – designing local interventions

The previous section took a strategic perspective on the application of sporting capital. In this section I examine the more localised implications of sporting capital theory for programme design and project implementation. What follows is an outline framework that in its specific implementation would need to be worked through with policy makers and practitioners as the programme design develops and is rolled out and as evaluative evidence is collected. However, as a starting point there are a number of areas where viewing programmes and their development through the sporting capital lens will potentially pay dividends as follows:

- In the targeting and recruitment process it is important to identify and understand the differences between those people with very low levels of sporting capital, those who come with modest levels and those who come with high levels as the intervention approach will need to be very different for each of these groups.

- Individuals with low sporting capital, and this will apply to many from disadvantaged backgrounds and particularly to young women, will require a focus that promotes and builds self efficacy, self confidence and potentially improves basic movement skills. The emphasis will need to be on intrinsic rather than extrinsic motivational factors and on reinforcing social networks. Psychological factors related to lack of confidence, self efficacy and negative body image will feature prominently in this group. The need for an empathetic environment and leadership style will be critical in addressing these factors. Building sporting capital in this group will be a slow process and individuals will be at high risk of an early drop out from the programme. Ideally they would receive one-to-one support and attention in the early stages and would benefit from mentoring from people who they see as like themselves.

- Those who come to a programme with higher levels of sporting capital may be participating at low levels because of negative external factors such as a lack of opportunity with few facilities or accessible clubs in their neighbourhood. They may face barriers relating to finance and cost and this will be the case for many living in areas of multiple deprivation. These individuals will benefit from the opportunity being made available to take part at a price they can afford. This group may include young people who have problems with authority and have had or are having difficulties at school. They may welcome more structured environments but ones that they are empowered to influence and that look different from the more authoritarian social contexts which make them feel uncomfortable and where they find it difficult to conform to expected behaviours. For this group competitive opportunities and the camaraderie of playing in teams can help to sustain and further build their sporting capital. People in this target market bring with them an aptitude for sport and may respond positively to the increased status that participation in sport can confer. They are candidates for using sport as the hook to engage them in more pro-social and educational activity and to develop their human capital through the transferable skills associated with voluntary involvement in sport.

- Some projects may go for a mix of recruits with varying levels of sporting capital but in so doing they need to take great care on how these groups interact and are provided for. The wrong mix can be counter-productive while the right mix can create empowered and positively reinforcing environments.
- Participation is invariably temporary while sporting capital is durable and associated with longer term engagement in sport. The focus of interventions needs to be on building sporting capital and not on increasing participation per se. This shifts the emphasis from judging success purely by attendance (which is a necessary condition) to judging success by the quality of the experience and the increase in sporting capital that accompanies it (i.e. sufficient conditions).
- Sporting capital is acquired through education and experience. Many young people in disadvantaged areas do not get the positive socialisation process that builds sporting capital in their early formative years. Many people young and not so young may come to the programme with what might be considered a 'sporting capital deficit'. The training and quality of sports leaders, mentors and coaches will be vital to the success of overcoming this deficit. They should be well versed in the ideas behind sporting capital and confident in applying the appropriate techniques and styles that will match the sporting capital levels of the people with which they are engaging. Some leaders and coaches may be better suited to work with people with high levels of sporting capital while others may be better suited to engaging with people with low levels, and it is important not to assume that one type of leader or coach fits all.

Figure 8.1 provides indicative guidance on the kind of response that may be appropriate based on an individual's overall Sporting Capital Index scores. This response would be shaped and modified further based on individual domain profiles and from learned experience of what works.

In this chapter I have endeavoured to build the bridge between theory, empirical evidence and policy and practice by starting to map out what a policy framework and implementation approach for community sport might look like when viewed through a 'sporting capital lens'. In so doing I have not attempted to write a comprehensive strategy, hardly appropriate in a book of this kind, nor have I been sufficiently presumptive as to dismiss outright all the years of cumulative experience that have led to the current strategic emphasis for sport in England and the programmes that support it. What I have suggested is that sporting capital theory would provide the central reference framework against which current policy initiatives and programmes could be 'audited' with a view to providing a joined up, logically coherent strategic approach that justifies where funding is directed, to whom, on what and in what ways that will deliver the desired outcome of

Sporting Capital Index score	Description	Intervention response
1 2 3	Individuals with these very low levels of sporting capital have a high probability of not participating in sport. They are more likely to be women than men, to be older rather than young and to come from lower socio-economic groups. They may have some underlying health problems and may have gone some time, in excess of a year for younger people and many years for those in older age groups, since they have taken part in any sport. They will not see themselves as 'sporty' and are likely to have low self esteem, and self confidence in relation to sport. Body image may be an issue for girls and young women in particular. Their physical abilities in sport will be relatively poor compared with their peers. They are likely to come from families that are not very sporty and few if any of their friends will be regular sport participants. They are unlikely to have visited any sporting venues in the recent past and are very unlikely to be a member of a sports club. They may find the idea of visiting a gym or sports centre intimidating. They will be a difficult group to attract to sporting programmes and will have a high probability of dropping out	This group is likely to be a minority market for national governing bodies of sport but are an important group for those concerned specifically with public health outcomes. They will require high intensity one-on-one support with a focus on psychological factors of self esteem and self confidence. Their motor skills may be weak and an emphasis on improving physical literacy will be important. Relatively low 'technically demanding' sports or adapted sports should be offered. This includes dance and fitness-related activities. They will not respond well to highly competitive environments and need a greater focus on task orientation and self referenced improvement. There should be an emphasis on enjoyment and fun. The initial introductory period will be crucial; it must be positive, non-threatening and rewarding. Positive feedback from project leaders is required. Building supportive social networks will be important. Group sessions should be with those on similar levels of sporting capital and single gender sessions are likely to be important for girls and women. Connections to other leisure and social activities where the individuals have greater confidence will help maintain involvement. Role models are likely to come from individuals who have started the programme with similar low levels of sporting capital and demonstrated increases. Success will be measured in terms of adherence to the programme and ultimately movement into a sporting capital level of 4 plus

Figure 8.1 Guidance on intervention design referenced to individual Sporting Capital Index scores

Sporting Capital Index score	Description	Intervention response
4 5 6 7	Individuals with these 'moderate' levels of sporting capital are likely to be positively disposed towards sport. They will have participated in a range of sports while at school but many have lacked the motivation to participate regularly since leaving school. Some will have dropped out temporarily with an intention to get back into sport when their personal circumstances change. They will have reasonable levels of self esteem and confidence in sporting situations but these may be fragile and prone to setbacks as a consequence of negative experiences. They will be sensitive to external barriers to participation prioritising other activities over sport and being easily persuaded 'not to bother to do sport today'. High cost (for them) and lack of access will be important deterring factors. Girls and young women in particular will be susceptible to peer group influence not to take part in sport. They are likely to come from families where at least some members are sporty and the value systems associated with sport are seen as positive.	This group is likely to be a core market for sports development and a key target population in a national strategy. These individuals will respond well to barrier reduction in terms for example of providing opportunities at the right cost, in the right place and at the right time. However psychological factors related to self-esteem and self confidence must not be taken for granted and require positive reinforcing environments for them to continue to be strengthened. This group may respond well to relatively low level competitive opportunities which need to be mixed with a focus on personal improvement and mastery of basic sporting skills. Some in this group will respond well to being coached and with the right support may be fast tracked into higher level performance programmes. Mixed gender sessions are a possibility – but should be with others on a similar sporting capital level. Building camaraderie and using existing friendship networks will be important to sustain the involvement of this group. Family connections to sport may be particularly helpful in recruiting those in their early teenage years. Success will be measured in levels of retention and ultimately in terms of progression to the 8 plus sporting capital group.

Figure 8.1 (Continued)

Sporting Capital Index score	Description	Intervention response
8 9 10	Individuals with these levels of sporting capital are already very sporty. They have a high probability of participating regularly in sport and to come back to sport following a short-term drop out. They will respond very positively to barrier reduction such as low cost opportunities and increased access or improved quality of facilities. If they are not already members of clubs they will be potential recruits. They are a target market for national governing bodies of sport and will respond well to technically demanding sports and to team sports. They are also potential volunteers and should be targeted for volunteer recruitment. They are often looking for improved opportunities to take part in competitive sport and in leagues and tournaments. They will respond well to coaching offers. Those with the highest sporting capital scores (9 or 10) may already be involved in high performance sport, identified as talented and engaged in talent development systems.	This population is relatively self-sufficient in terms of having a high probability of meeting their own sporting needs. Life-stage is an important factor influencing the participation of this group. At the lower end of the spectrum, a Score of 8, they are more prone to dropping out if life circumstances get in the way of their sport. To this extent it is a mistake to take participation amongst this group for granted. Although providing the core market place for national governing bodies this group will not feature as a priority for publically subsidised interventions trying to extend the sport participation market. Their involvement in such programmes and projects should be welcome as long as they do not crowd out or jeopardise success with the other priority markets with lower levels of sporting capital. These kinds of individuals are a potential market for sports club membership and for recruitment into volunteering. The focus for this group is on 'participation maintenance'. Continued quality experiences will help reinforce their already positive attitudes towards sport. It is amongst this group that the potential Olympic champions of the future are most likely to be identified.

Figure 8.1 (Continued)

increasing sporting capital across the population. In so doing gaps will be identified, some traditional ideas that support investment may be dropped, others may be given more emphasis or priority while others may be adapted and yet other completely innovative approaches might emerge. To draw an analogy, sporting capital would provide the 'big picture' on the box of the jigsaw puzzle that would make the process of identifying the pieces and joining them up much easier to achieve. Viewed in this way sporting capital theory provides both a vision of what community sport might look like in terms of painting a new big picture on the box and would change the nature and relationship of the pieces of the puzzle and the process of fitting them together.

References

Bouchal, P. and Norris, E., n.d. *Implementing sure start children's centres*. Joseph Rowntree Foundation and Institute for Government. Available at: <www.instituteforgovernment.org.uk/sites/default/files/publications/Implementing%20Sure%20Start%20Childrens%20Centres%20-%20final_0.pdf> [accessed 27th June 2017].

Cavill, N. and Baumann, A., 2004. Changing the way people think about health-enhancing physical activity: Do mass media campaigns have a role? *Journal of Sports Sciences*, 22(8), pp. 771–790.

Collins, M., 1988. *Discussion on campaigns*. Unpublished internal communication while Head of Research at Sport England. Included in slide presentation by Rowe, N. 'Sports Council campaigns- the lessons learned – a cautionary tale'. Presentation originally prepared by Nick Rowe in 1998 and updated 2003.

Department of Health, 2011. *Start active, stay active: A report on physical activity from the four home countries' Chief Medical Officers*. London: H.M. Government.

H. M. Government, 2015. *Sporting future: A new strategy for an active nation*. London: Cabinet Office.

Houlihan, B. and White, A., 2002. *The politics of sport development: Development of sport or development through sport?* London: Routledge.

Let's Move! Child Care, n.d. Available at: <https://healthykidshealthyfuture.org> [accessed 14th June 2017].

Mills, C. W., 1959. *The sociological imagination*. London: Oxford University Press.

Shape America, n.d. Available at: <www.shapeamerica.org/about> [accessed 14th June 2017].

Sport England, 2016. *Sport England: Towards an active nation, strategy 2016–2021*. London: Sport England.

Sport England, 2017. *This girl can*. Available at: <www.sportengland.org/our-work/women/this-girl-can>.

UK Active, n.d. *Start young, stay active*. Childhood Physical Literacy Report. Available at: <www.ukactive.com/downloads/managed/Start_Young_Stay_Active.pdf> [accessed 18th June 2017].

Youth Sport Trust, n.d. *Primary school physical literacy framework*. Available at: <www.youthsporttrust.org/sites/yst/files/resources/documents/physical_literacy_framework.pdf> [accessed 18th June 2017].

Youth Sport Trust, 2017. *Early years physical literacy framework*. Available at: <www.activematters.org/uploads/pdfs/PLF_APRIL_2017.pdf> [accessed 18th June 2017].

Where do we go from here? Applying, refining and testing the model of sporting capital

In this final chapter I weave a number of threads together to summarise what we have learned about sporting capital, its relationship to participation in sport and its potential as a theoretical framework to inform sport policy and practice. Looking forward, I recommend an ongoing programme of research that will further refine and test the theory which I have acknowledged is in its infancy. However, in so doing I take the position that the plausibility of the theory and the evidence presented so far provides a sufficiently strong argument to immediately view sports development through a sporting capital lens and to start building strategy and policy informed by the vision, principles and propositions that it espouses. So by way of summary, what are those propositions and what are the areas of research that would help to test, refine and further develop the theory?

Sporting capital is defined as, *"the stock of physiological, sociological and psychological attributes and competencies that support and motivate an individual to participate in sport and to sustain that participation over time."* The key propositions of sporting capital theory may be summarised as follows:

- That participation in sport is a product and expression of a number of capacities that an individual holds. Those capacities take the form of physiological attributes to include both physical health and physical competency; psychological attributes of self esteem, self confidence, self efficacy and identity; and social connections made up of interpersonal relationships with family friends and significant others in sport.
- The physiological, psychological and social connections in sport may be conceptualised as three separate but closely interrelated domains that, working in combination, make up an individual's overall level of sporting capital.
- Sporting capital is analogous to human capital and closely related to social and cultural capital. The nature of these capitals is that there is transferability across them; so, for example, given the right conditions,

increases in sporting capital can facilitate and increase human, cultural and/or social capital and vice versa.

- Although focused on individual capacities and underpinned by an empowering philosophy, sporting capital is shaped and influenced by the socio-political and cultural context in which a person lives. These contexts have both a national and local dimension. To this extent we would expect to see structural inequalities in the levels and distribution of sporting capital across different socio-cultural groups in society that are similar if not precisely the same as we see for participation in sport.

- Sporting capital is a universal idea that has relevance at a number of geographical levels from neighbourhoods, to local communities, to nations and international comparisons. Although it will vary from individual to individual and from place to place, the basic building blocks of sporting capital remain the same even though contexts will change.

- Sporting capital is directly related to levels and frequencies of participation in sport and through sport has the potential to increase individual physical and mental health and in aggregate benefit public health outcomes. The higher the levels of sporting capital, the higher the probability of regular and sustained participation in sport and the lower the probability of drop out.

- Levels of sporting capital not only determine the likelihood of current participation but also impact on the probability that it will be sustained into later life. People with high levels of sporting capital are much more likely to engage in lifelong participation than their peers with low levels of sporting capital.

- Sporting capital may be thought of as an invisible 'stock' of attributes or capabilities that an individual carries around with them. The visible expression of sporting capital is in the act of participating. It is expected that an individual with high levels of sporting capital will be confident in themselves physically, will be comfortable in the social situations in which sport takes place and will demonstrate a sufficient level of skill and physicality that will make the activity of taking part engaging and rewarding.

- The higher levels of sporting capital an individual has, the greater potential for that individual to fully enjoy the experience of taking part in sport. Such experiences open up the opportunity for self actualisation and self expression leading to greater happiness and improved quality of life. This operates as a virtuous circle with increases in sporting capital increasing the potential for enjoyment which in turn further increases sporting capital.

- Sporting capital is more stable and durable than participation behaviours which are prone to fragility, high levels of churn and to short or sustained periods of drop out. Although sporting capital is relatively stable, an individual's 'stock' is prone to attrition over time and with increased 'distance' from sport associated with extended periods of drop out and sedentary behaviours.

- Individual levels of sporting capital are directly related to the levels of motivation to take part in sport which in turn impacts on the likelihood of overcoming the constraints and barriers faced at different stages in a person's life. In this sense external barriers to participation are not absolute or objectively defined but are relative to an individual's level of sporting capital.

- The quality of experience an individual has when participating impacts on their levels of sporting capital. A high quality experience that is perceived to be enjoyable will serve to maintain or build the stock of sporting capital the more it is 'used', while repeated mediocre experiences will over time degrade levels of sporting capital and eventually lead to drop out. At the extreme, a traumatic one-off negative experience could lead to a catastrophic decline in levels of sporting capital with significant negative consequences for participation.

- Socialisation processes from birth impact on an individual's level of sporting capital. In the earliest years parents and siblings are the greatest influence, but as children get older influences widen into the school and community environment. The teenage years provide an important stage in sporting capital development with peer influences becoming more significant than family ones. The process of maturation and identity development through adolescence can either reinforce or undermine sporting capital.

- Although early years' experience is a crucial period for building sporting capital, it is possible with the right quality experience and support to build sporting capital at any stage in a person's life.

- Different sports because of their varying technical, physical and social demands place different demands on levels of sporting capital. Some sports – unless adapted from their traditional forms – are likely only to appeal to individuals with high levels of sporting capital, while other less 'demanding' sports may prove more attractive as an entry point back into sport for those on low levels of sporting capital.

- Matching intervention design and types of delivery mechanisms to individual levels of sporting capital will maximise the probability of successful outcomes. These outcomes will be defined in terms of increases in individual levels of sporting capital rather than in terms of attendance and participation behaviours alone.

The empirical research reported in this book has provided insight and evidence that informs a number of the above propositions. Through the construction of a Sporting Capital Index it has demonstrated a direct relationship between levels of sporting capital and the probability of participating in sport. Importantly, it has shown that this relationship is not a straight line one but one in which as levels of sporting capital increase the probability of participating in sport increases at a faster rate. The empirical evidence has also shown how sporting capital is differentially distributed across the population by age, gender and social class. It shows how the antecedents to participation in the form of the psychological, physiological and social domains that go to make up sporting capital are structurally divided in society and suggests the link to socialisation processes that impact on these inequalities. The profiling of levels of sporting capital by frequency of participation and types of sports has shown that these are related and that what we consider to be some of our major participant sports are likely to appeal only to a narrow range of individuals with high levels of sporting capital.

These are all important findings and serve to add rather than in any way to diminish the theoretical explanatory strength of sporting capital. However, it does still leave many of the above propositions untested empirically, albeit we have seen in Chapter 4 how much of the theoretical thinking underpinning sporting capital is informed by and consistent with other theories of behaviour change that have undergone extensive research scrutiny. We have also seen in Chapter 5 how a review of research evidence on the factors and experiences that impact on sports participation across the life-course make sense when examined through the lens of sporting capital and certainly do not contradict any aspects of the theory.

The need for 'strategic' research: improving our measurement and understanding of the theory of sporting capital

What further research is required to test the key propositions underpinning the theory? I would propose a number of approaches which are not mutually exclusive and may be carried out in parallel or in a mixed method integrated research programme as follows:

- **Methodological focused research** to further apply, and test the Sporting Capital Index (SCI) to establish the reliability and validity of the measures used and the potential to develop and refine the model to improve its explanatory power. In the process the sensitivity of different measures as they impact on the overall outcomes could be tested. Methodological research could also be extended to develop and test measures of sporting capital as they might apply to people with a disability. This would explore what, if any, differences in theoretical perspectives and measurement processes might apply in this context. Ideally objective measures of physical competence would be developed and incorporated into the model to differentiate them from perceived competence. Further research is required to develop practical and cost effective objective measures of non-sport specific fundamental motor skills targeted particularly but not exclusively at primary- and secondary-aged young people that in their case could be applied in school settings. Objective measures of physical competence would support both improved SCI measures of sporting capital and provide benchmark measures against which progress in a range of basic sport-related skill areas could be assessed. More generally, the SCI presented in this book has been developed for application with adults aged 16 years and over. Methodological research is required to explore how these measures could be developed to extend the SCI to younger age populations.

- **Cross sectional empirical research** at different geographies from neighbourhood to local communities to comparative international research. At a local level research would establish how much variation there is in the levels of sporting capital from place to place and what neighbourhood and local community factors impact on these levels. Comparing sporting capital levels and profiles between neighbourhoods and communities in urban and rural settings with different population densities matched by affluence, poverty, social class and diversity would allow us to explore what public policy and environmental factors, if any, make a difference. Factors that might emerge as influential differentiators include the nature of the school environments; the quality and level of provision, the investment in sports development, access to safe high quality open spaces and play environments; the strength of social and community sport networks; the predominant styles of management of public facilities and availability and targeting of concessions, and the nature of transport systems and road layouts. At an international comparative level the research would require a collaborative effort across countries to both benchmark levels of sporting capital and explore its relationship to participation in sport in those countries. It would be expected that countries like Sweden, Norway, Finland and Denmark with relatively high levels of participation in sport when compared with those in England and the rest of the UK would have higher levels of sporting capital. But it is not clear how much higher sporting capital is in these countries and how it differs in its distribution across different sectors of the population, particularly in terms of age, gender and class. Once differences are established, it would be possible to start exploring causative factors that include family cultures, educational contexts including pre-school experiences and settings, community provision, sporting networks and club environments, access and economic factors of price and affordability, and government policies and interventions as well as broader socio-cultural contexts.
- **Longitudinal research.** The above research would still be limited by its cross sectional nature. As we have seen in earlier chapters, sporting

capital is by definition a dynamic theory that involves individual change and development over time. Figure 3.3 in Chapter 3 encapsulated the temporal qualities in the interaction between sporting capital levels and barriers to participation. Figure 3.4 presents a dynamic system in a continuous state of change as the experience of participation impacts on sporting capital levels which impact on motivation to participate which is mediated through barriers and constraints to impact on the experience of participation which again impacts on sporting capital levels and so on. Although relatively durable, an individual's level of sporting capital is never static; it is either growing through a feedback loop of positive experiences, decreasing through negative experiences or it is slowly undergoing attrition with inactivity. The evidence for the impact of early learning experiences with the influence of family, peers and significant others on participation is extensive, as shown in Chapter 5; however, further longitudinal designed research is required to understand the processes by which sporting capital is built, the points in the formative experiences of young people's lives when their sporting capital levels diverge and why. Longitudinal research could explore how important parents, families, peers, teachers, coaches or significant others are in influencing an individual's levels of sporting capital at what age and in what settings. Research could further explore how these experiences are affected by gender, class, ethnicity and disability to better understand the nature of the interaction and relative impact of external barriers and constraints on levels of sporting capital and participation rates in sport. Extending research to older people, the durability of sporting capital through the life-course could be explored to better understand the impact of life transitions, what levels of sporting capital are required to be resilient to what types of constraints and barriers, and how sporting capital impacts on re-entry into sport after extended periods of drop out.

- **Qualitative research.** In addition to empirical research there is a need for complementary qualitative research designed to better explore the meaning of sporting capital as understood and experienced by people with low, moderate and high levels. I referred earlier in this book to how difficult it is for people with high levels of sporting capital (which makes up most of those working in sports development) to have empathy with those on low levels to fully understand what it feels like to be 'in their shoes'. What does the 'sporting world' and the people who take part in it look like through the eyes of someone who finds doing physical things difficult, being physically active or playing sport potentially embarrassing and are self conscious or feel intimidated or threatened in sporting settings or situations? How do people see their own sporting biography and the significant points of influence in that biography that either turned them off or onto sport? Is sporting capital with its three domains something they can understand and relate to and how would they describe it in their own words? Does the theory translate into their lived experiences of sport and do the propositions make sense to them? Do they believe that it is possible to build their own sporting capital no matter how low the starting point and what if anything would make them interested in trying? For parents of young children, to what extent do they feel they can make a difference to their child's level of sporting capital and how do they reflect on any conscious or potentially unconscious biases they may have as a consequence of, for example, gender-defined expectations and stereotypes?

Intervention-based programme evaluation – what works to build sporting capital?

The above research designs are exploratory approaches that seek to improve our measurement and understanding of the theory of sporting capital, to test its explanatory power and, if necessary, to refine its propositions. In the process the learning from such research would have important practical benefits for policy makers and practitioners. However, in addition to the above 'strategic' research, there is a strong argument to support a national programme of intervention-based research that is designed to test the 'on the ground' efficacy of different types and styles of intervention, involving collaborative effort between national and local policy makers, practitioners, academic and other commissioned researchers in think tanks, market research agencies and management consultancies. This *research-led programme evaluation* rather than the *programme-led research evaluation*, which has been the normal practice, would support the move away from the 'shopping list' programme design mentality referred to earlier in this book towards a rational evidence-informed framework for public policy intervention.

The gold standard experimental research design is using randomised control trials (RCTs) with tightly defined intervention 'treatments' and outcomes measured against control groups not subject to the intervention but matched in every other way. However, as Chatterji (2016, p. 129) points out,

> experimental designs (particularly, RCTs) are extremely difficult to mount and sustain in real world settings for investigating any kind of social intervention, let alone CSPs (Complex Social Problems). Numerous assumptions underlying experiments tend to become violated under field conditions . . . complex programs are difficult to manipulate experimentally; initial randomization of subjects to treatment and control

conditions is frequently compromised due to participant mobility or nonparticipation; environmental contamination of various types are a real threat, and issues of multiple causation – where more than one program influences the targeted outcomes in a given population – could potentially yield confounded, contradictory or un-interpretable effects.

There is wide consensus today in the evaluation community that programme-theory-driven evaluation is a pragmatic and useful way to deal with the complexity of community-based interventions designed to achieve behavioural outcomes (see Chen, 1989; Weiss, 1995, 1997; Pawson and Tilley, 1997; Pawson, 2006; Donaldson, 2007). As Coalter (2007, p. 2) in his critique of the evidence informing public policy and practice in sport states,

> there is an emerging view that *the* major methodological limitation on producing evidence for policy making and practice is the absence of an understanding or processes and mechanisms which either produce, or are assumed to produce particular impacts and outcomes.

A research design focused on testing the theory of sporting capital fits well with a 'realistic (or realist) evaluation' approach as promoted by Pawson and Tilley (1997). A realist approach assumes that whenever a programme is implemented, it is testing a theory about what 'might cause change', even though that theory may not be explicit. One of the tasks of a realist evaluation is therefore to make the theories within a programme explicit, by developing clear hypotheses about how, and for whom, programmes might 'work'. The implementation of the programme, and the evaluation of it, then tests those hypotheses. This means collecting data, not just about programme impacts, or the processes of programme implementation, but about the specific aspects of programme context that might impact on programme outcomes, and about the specific mechanisms that might be creating change. A realist evaluation approach to research design recognises the inevitable 'noise' that surrounds project interventions that seek to achieve behavioural change outcomes. It looks for mechanisms and balances of probability of causality in differing contexts that provide sufficient evidence to support the investment of public money and the appropriate transferability of learning. Pawson and Tilley (1997) argue that a realist approach has particular implications for the design of an evaluation and the roles of participants. For example, rather than comparing changes for participants who have undertaken a programme with a group of people who have not (as is in an RCT or quasi-experimental design), a realist evaluation compares mechanisms and outcomes within programmes. It may ask, for example, whether a programme works differently in different localities (and if so, how and why); or for different population groups (for example, men and women, or groups with differing socio-economic status). Everitt (1996, p. 177) goes so far as to propose that "The aim of evaluation . . . is not 'to establish whether there is a cause-effect relationship', but to judge merit. In other words, to judge whether the practice is 'good', 'good enough', 'poor' or 'corrupt'".

A realistic evaluation research design requires stakeholders to make explicit the theory of change that underpins their intervention through the development of a programme 'logic model'. A logic model shows how programme design and delivery (inputs and activities) are linked by a range of mechanisms to achieve desired programme outcomes in different contexts. Making this theory of change explicit in the form of a logic model challenges stakeholders to think through what they are doing, why they are doing what they are doing and how by doing these things in different contexts they will achieve the desired outcomes. Chen (1989, p. 391) refers to this stage of theory driven intervention design as 'normative theory' that

> provides the rationale and justification for the program structure . . . . .
> providing guidance for issues such as what kinds of goals the program
> should pursue, what kinds of treatments should be formulated, and
> what kind of implementation procedures and processes will be required.

This is distinguished from, "causal theory that specifies the underlying causal mechanisms which link, mediate or condition the causal relationships between the treatment variables and the outcome variables in the program." (Chen, 1989, p. 392)

Sporting capital by definition is a theory of change and as we have seen in Chapter 3 has an inherent logic model that informs both 'normative' programme design and 'causative' links between 'treatment' and 'outcome'. I have already noted that it is a theory that is in its infancy and like all theories its description and interpretation of the 'real world' and, most importantly, its contribution to effective practice will need to be tested, refuted, supported and more than likely refined over time based on the evidence from experience 'on the ground'. The evidence gained from a realist intervention research design can contribute towards more effective policy and practice through shared learning and understanding. Figure 9.1 shows an adapted version of the logic model presented in Chapter 3 that applies a sporting capital 'theory of change' to programme intervention. As with most logic models the time progression is from left to right with the exception of the intervention focused on barrier reduction which may happen concurrently or even in advance of the interventions focused on building sporting capital. A brief explanation is given below of each stage

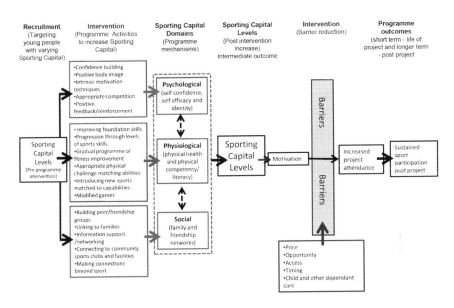

Figure 9.1 Project intervention logic model: building sporting capital

in the logic model as it would be applied to sporting capital informed and structured interventions.

- **Pre intervention recruitment – targeting people with varying levels of sporting capital.** The model begins with the recruitment process. This aspect of programme intervention is often overlooked or given insufficient priority and yet it is critical to the final impact and achievement of desired programme outcomes. Too many programmes are doomed to limited impact from the start because they do not attract their target market. In the case of sport programmes aimed at increasing participation amongst low participant groups (those with low levels of sporting capital), they too often attract too many from those who already participate without the support of the intervention. To be effective, different recruitment strategies will be required for people in different circumstances and with different levels of sporting capital. Establishing the sporting capital levels of people recruited onto the programme will provide a measure of the effectiveness of projects hitting target markets and the benchmark from which impact can be assessed.
- **Intervention – programme activities to increase sporting capital.** Once recruited, project participants are exposed to the programme activities

that are designed to increase levels of sporting capital. These impact on sporting capital levels through the three domains: the psychological, physiological and social domains which are the mechanisms for eliciting change. The list of intervention activities provided in Figure 9.1 is indicative and drawn from the guidance set out in Figure 8.1 in the previous chapter. It should not be considered exhaustive, with project managers, leaders and coaches all to be encouraged through an evolving process to find innovative activities and ways of working that engage people to build their sporting capital. Ideally the style and intervention strategies will be tailored to the specific needs of the individual based on the sporting capital profiling that is carried out for new recruits focusing on building on their strengths and overcoming their weaknesses.

• **Post intervention – increases in sporting capital levels – short term over the life of the project.** Measuring sporting capital at stages during the intervention will provide the test of how effective the project has been in increasing levels of sporting capital for each individual separately and for groups of individuals (e.g. recent school leavers; women; young people at risk of offending; the most deprived' people at various life-stages and transitions) and in aggregate across the project as a whole. With increasing sporting capital individuals will be more likely to have a good attendance record as sport becomes a more enjoyable, less threatening and a more fulfilling activity; as physical abilities improve and fitness levels increase; and as social networks strengthen around sport. Regular attendance is an important intermediate measure of success as attendance (i.e. increased contact time) is a necessary (but importantly not sufficient) condition of longer term success in building sporting capital and sustaining participation behaviour change through the life-course. This is seen as an intermediate measure on the road to achieving the ultimate outcome of increased sustained participation in sport. The measurement of intervention impact on sporting capital may take place on a number of occasions during the life of the project for any given individual, providing the opportunity for feedback that can be used to refine and modify the intervention approach taken with them. Intermediate measures of improved self efficacy, self confidence, basic skill acquisition and positive measures of social integration and strengthened social networks around sport will help track individual progress and will help understand what aspects of the intervention design are working and in what ways.

• **Programme outcome – longer term post project intervention.** The ultimate outcome (from a sport perspective – but an intermediate outcome in terms of the wider health, community and economic benefits that sport can bring) is significant increases in sporting capital that support sustained increases in participation in sport for individuals once they have left the intervention. Although it will not be possible to assess whether the intervention has achieved behaviour change that will support a 'sporting habit for life', it is important to assess whether sustained changes in participation have taken place within a reasonable time-frame (6 months to one year) post project intervention and to test the hypothesised correlation with sporting capital levels. Evidence of sustained behaviour change 6 to 12 months post project attendance will increase confidence that longer lasting lifetime changes have taken place.

- **Intervention to reduce barriers.** Reducing barriers will be an important part of any intervention and will particularly be the case for people from disadvantaged backgrounds. For those with high levels of sporting capital, reducing barriers may be enough on its own to ensure attendance at projects and provide the foundation that will support sustained participation. However, for many people with moderate and low levels of sporting capital, barrier reduction alone will not be sufficient to attract them to attend projects, to keep them engaged once they have attended or to provide them with the capacities and motivation to continue participating once they leave. Effective projects will strike the right balance between reducing barriers and building sporting capital and will tailor their response in ways that are sensitive to individual requirements and experience. Exploring how that balance is derived and successfully implemented will be a key part of the evaluation and the shared learning that emerges from it.

The realistic research design described above would involve a range of measurement protocols to track the relationship between process, mechanisms and outcomes. The crucial measurement would be that of profiling sporting capital levels of those recruited onto the programme and then measured at various stages during its life to track individual and in aggregate project-wide impacts. The existing protocols for measuring sporting capital presented in Chapter 3 and providing the empirical evidence to build the Sporting Capital Index are available to apply 'off the shelf' (see Nordern, 2013) to provide individual profiling in project and programme settings. These could be further refined and tested as part of the evaluation process and to support the methodological research discussed earlier. In addition to quantitative methods, qualitative research designs would need to be incorporated into the evaluation focused on the project providers (the agents of change referred to in Chapter 8) operating in both strategic and front line delivery roles and the project participants. The outcome would be a synthesis of evidence that would inform project success (or more correctly probabilities of success) by understanding process mechanisms and outcomes referenced against an understood theory of change (Figure 9.2).

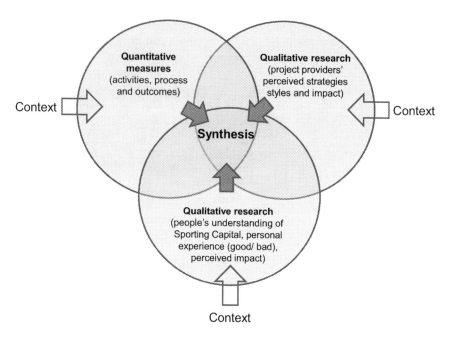

Figure 9.2 A multi-method approach to project evaluation

Sporting capital – where do we go from here?

As important as it is, I did not want the last words in this book to be concerned with details on the design of intervention strategies informed by sporting capital theory. I started this book by saying that it is about an idea conceptualised in two simple words 'sporting capital'. Although my fundamental thoughts on the nature of sporting capital, its component domains and propositions that follow from it had already been formed before embarking on this exercise, they have in the process of writing this book been constantly challenged and re-assessed. My ideas have as a consequence developed but have not been fundamentally changed. I still believe that sporting capital provides the potential to fill a theoretical void in community sports development that could provide a unifying opportunity for transformative change. I am conscious that such bold claims are there to be challenged and knocked down and I understand the implicit criticism many might feel who have conscientiously worked in community sports development and have undoubtedly achieved many good things. I have not absolved myself from that association and responsibility as modest as my contribution may have been. My intention in this book is not, however, to dwell on or be critical of the past but to position sporting capital as a theory about the future. In many instances it is about taking forward those good practices that already exist that are consistent with the theory, while in other cases it is about challenging conventional wisdom, normal ways of working and what might be misplaced priorities. I return in the end, however, to the humanising nature of the theory. It is a theory about capability and not deficit. It sees sport participation as a form of empowerment, a source of joy, pleasure and self expression that should be made possible for everyone no matter what their age, gender, ethnicity, disability, economic circumstances or social background. My hope is that having read this book you share my optimism that sporting capital can make a difference and whatever your walk of life you become an advocate for it.

References

Chatterji, M., 2016. Causal inferences on the effectiveness of complex social programs: Navigating assumptions, sources of complexity and evaluation design challenges. *Evaluation and Program Planning*, 59, pp. 128–140.

Chen, H. T., 1989. The conceptual framework of the theory-driven perspective. *Evaluation and Program Planning*, 12, pp. 391–396.

Coalter, F., 2007. *A wider social role for sport: Who's keeping the score.* London: Routledge.

Donaldson, S. I., 2007. *Program theory-driven evaluation science.* New York: Lawrence Erlbaum.

Everitt, A., 1996. Developing critical evaluation. *Evaluation*, 2(2), pp. 173–188.

Nordern, O., 2013. *Creating sporting capital scores: Technical document.* London: BMRB.

Pawson, R., 2006. *Evidence-based policy: A realist perspective.* London: Sage.

Pawson, R. and Tilley, N., 1997. *Realistic evaluation.* London: Sage.

Weiss, C. H., 1995. Nothing as practical as a good theory: Exploring theory-based evaluation for comprehensive community initiatives for children and families. In: J. P. Connell, A. C. Kubisch, L. B. Schorr, and C. H. Weiss, eds. *New approaches to evaluating community initiatives, vol. 1: Concepts, methods, and contexts.* New York: Aspen Institute, pp. 65–92.

Weiss, C. H., 1997. How can theory-based evaluation make greater headway? *Evaluation Review*, 21(4), pp. 501–524.

Index

Page numbers in italic indicate figures on the corresponding pages

Printed in the United States
By Bookmasters